FLOATING PALACES
THE GREAT ATLANTIC LINERS

D1341314

The author became fascinated by the great liners, such as the *Liberte*, in the 1950s as they passed before him along the Hoboken, New Jersey, waterfront. The Hudson River was the great stage set and the splendid skyline of Manhattan was the scenery. It was a fantastic maritime production. (Author's Collection)

FLOATING PALACES
THE GREAT ATLANTIC LINERS

William H. Miller

AMBERLEY

for Anthony La Forgia

*dear friend, fellow Hobokenite & great fan
of the great liners*

First published 2010, this edition 2015

Amberley Publishing
The Hill, Stroud
Gloucestershire, GL5 4EP

www.amberley-books.com

ISBN 978 1 4456 5047 0 (print)
ISBN 978 1 4456 2344 3 (ebook)

British Library Cataloguing in Publication Data.
A catalogue record for this book is available from the British Library.

Typeset in 11pt on 12pt Sabon LT Std.
Typesetting by Amberley Publishing.
Printed in the UK.

The great Hudson River was a near-constant parade of ships, both large and
small. (Author's Collection)

CONTENTS

FOREWORD

In November 2010, I sailed westbound on the *Queen Mary 2*, from Southampton to New York. It was my very first trip on that great and grand Cunarder, in many ways a ship that continues the legacy of the Floating Palaces. Yes, the *Queen Mary 2* is a floating palace, a modern, amenity-filled, creature-comfortable, even user-friendly floating palace. The food, the service, the entertainment and, of course, the sheer ambience were wonderful. I left the ship ready to book another voyage on that 151,000-ton flagship of a renewed, bigger and, in ways, better Cunard Line.

A great highlight of that voyage was having my good friend Bill Miller aboard and as lecturer. Bill is aptly called 'Mr Ocean Liner'. He is, as I continue to realize, much like an evangelist, the 'Billy Graham of ocean liners'. He spreads the word, tells the rich story and equally shares the rich history of the great ocean liners. He shows people. He teaches. And he himself is, in his almost mesmerizing, engulfing style, even bigger in ways than the oversized historic photos that appear on the big screen next to him. He has, it seems, unbridled enthusiasm, quick wit, certainly high energy. For each of his lectures, he filled each and every seat of Illuminations, the ship's 600-capacity planetarium–theatre. The setting, so appropriate and so appropriately glamorous, is pure 'ocean liner style' or, as Bill would say, 'so Fred & Ginger'. It is contemporary art deco, the great 1930s cinema palace, the Odeon at sea!

The grand liners, like leading ladies themselves, appear vividly in Bill's talks. The likes of the *Mauretania*, *Titanic*, *Ile de France*, *Normandie*, *Queen Mary* and the *United States* flashed on that enormous screen. There were also scenes of luxurious interiors, immigrants in steerage, soldier-passengers in wartime and even a slight mention of tragedy, such as the burnt out, capsized *Normandie*. The audience, including the most mildly curious and lightly interested, were soon transfixed, drawn in, happily joining the ranks of 'the converted'. Afterward, Bill hurried to the ship's book shop-library to sign copies of his many books.

Like many others, I am very grateful to Bill for keeping the subject of ocean liners alive and well – and making them interesting, even fascinating. I love liners too and my personal favorites are the *Olympic*, *Queen Mary* and, although somewhat smaller, the *Caronia* of 1948, the illustrious 'Green Goddess' of Cunard. I am fascinated with their roles in the twentieth century. My contribution of sorts is to collect, share and, most of all, sell ocean liner memorabilia (through www.luxurylinerrow.com).

In this book, Bill has given yet another treat: the story of these liners, ever fascinating and with often unpublished photos and an evocative text. Three blasts to Bill – and to the Floating Palaces, that great cast of the greatest Atlantic liners!

Brian Hawley
Winterville, North Carolina
December 2010

INTRODUCTION

On an otherwise warm summer's afternoon, my friend Tony La Forgia and I had lunch together at a small restaurant in the back streets of Hoboken, the New Jersey community in which we were both born and raised. The air was warm and still, the rows of trees hanging limp and almost lifeless. But the pace of that mile-square city remained brisk. We were not far from the Hudson River, from the waterfront that made Hoboken famous and from the last of the great piers just across the Hudson River and over in New York City. It had changed, of course, and much of the past (such as the great piers themselves) was gone. Even if slightly, however, we could feel a connection; that link to the past. Exactly the same age, we also both adore ocean liners. We spoke that day, as always, of the great liners, those grand ships of bygone days. Our memories were and remain rich and full.

Just blocks from our luncheon, the Hoboken waterfront was once home to some of the world's largest and grandest liners – ships such as the turn-of-the-century German four-stackers and to even bigger ships such as the *Imperator* and the *Vaterland*. Later, in the First World War, great numbers of troops passed through the Hoboken piers bound for the trenches of Europe, to fight the armies of the German Kaiser and aboard many confiscated German ships. In the early 1930s, ships such as the *Aquitania* and *Mauretania* berthed in Hoboken for a short time. Later, in 1934–38, the giant *Leviathan* sat out her final days rusting and silent at the Third Street pier, a sad victim of the Depression. Yes, our nearness to the Hoboken waterfront was a connection of

sorts to these great ships, the Floating Palaces, and to the grand age of the Atlantic liners.

These days, the greatest legacy of the great liners, those 'castles of the sea', is more of the glamorous and luxurious image they have left behind. *Floating Palaces: The Great Atlantic Liners* is the most popular lecture I give aboard modern-day cruise ships as well as on the nostalgic crossings of the Cunard liners, especially the *Queen Mary 2*. The ships, from the likes of the *Mauretania* and the *Titanic*, the *Ile de France* and the original *Queen Mary*, are woven into history as well. They were part of world affairs and social as well as cultural changes. The link is rich.

And even with the immense creature comforts of contemporary cruise ships, all of them indeed akin to floating resorts, nostalgic readers of ocean liner history books and loyal attendees at lectures somehow still yearn for the glamour and style and sheer magic of those bygone floating palaces. Crossings on the Atlantic were, of course, different – with a different purpose. But there is the everlasting image of, say, Marlene Dietrich, swathed in furs and laden with fine jewels, poised on the deck of the magnificent *Normandie*. She was heading for a summer in Europe with thirty-eight trunks! And there's also the rich lore of the 275 items on a first class dinner menu on board the *Ile de France*, dog menus and top-deck kennels that included miniature New York City fire hydrants and millionaires reserving their favorite suites for years ahead. Yes, it was all magic.

I am writing this Introduction on a bright summer's morning quite near New York City. A day later, I will sail aboard the mighty *Queen Mary 2* as a guest lecturer. Some of the passengers will come to my first talk, almost always about the floating palaces, that evocative overview of twentieth-century, transatlantic liner travel. That talk has actually inspired, sparked this book.

This work is an overview, a grand review, of some of the greatest, largest and fastest Atlantic liners. Indeed, they were aptly named – the Floating Palaces. Now, the steam whistles are screeching into a moodful, foggy afternoon and we are about to sail off, on another journey of words and pictures.

Bill Miller
Secaucus, New Jersey
June 2010

ACKNOWLEDGMENTS

Assembling a book takes many hands, a full 'crew'. As the author, I direct from the 'wheelhouse' – deciding on the chapter titles, organizing the text, assembling the photos. But the 'crew' is so tremendously important and much appreciated. Firstly, I would like to specially thank Campbell McCutcheon and Amberley Publishing for suggesting and then taking on this title. Added thanks to Janette McCutcheon for sharing the family ocean liner collection.

Very special appreciation to those splendid maritime artists: Stephen Card, James Flood, Robert Lloyd, William Muller, Hayao Nogami, Don Stoltenberg and the late Joseph Wilhelm.

Further thanks must go to the late Frank Andrews, Dr Nelson Arnstein, the late Frank Braynard, Tom Cassidy, Anthony Cooke, Luis Miguel Correia, the Cronican-Arroyo Collection, Maurizio Eliseo, Sir Harold Evans, Richard Faber, John Ferguson, Howard Franklin, Michael Hadgis, Brian Hawley, John Heywood, Pine Hodges, Charles Howland, Norman Knebel, the late Vincent Messina, Robert Neal Marshall, the late Abe Michaelson, Hisashi Noma, Mary Pelzer, Mario Pulice, the late James Sesta, the late Der Scutt, John Tabbut-McCarthy, the late Everett Viez, Robert Welding, Al Wilhelmi and Jay Wolff.

Organizations that have assisted include British Airways, Canadian Pacific Steamships, Crystal Cruises, Cunard Line, French Line, Hapag-Lloyd, Holland America Line, Hotel Queen Mary, Moran Towing & Transport Company, Port Authority of New York & New Jersey, Seaport Museum of New York, Silversea Cruises, *South China Morning News*, Steamship Historical Society of America, United States Lines, World Ocean & Cruise Liner Society and the World Ship Society, especially the Port of New York Branch.

My humble apologies if anyone has been incorrectly overlooked.

THE GERMANS &
THE FIRST FLOATING PALACES

These days, you can stroll through beautifully created parkland along the famed waterfront of Hoboken, New Jersey. There are trees, walking paths, playgrounds, dog runs and of course panoramic views of the great New York City skyline. The mighty Hudson River, still busy with ferries and tugs and barges and the occasional passing cruise ship, is the divide. Cool breezes often add to the setting. It is all part of the great restoration and redevelopment not just of the Hoboken waterfront, but along the Manhattan and more distant Brooklyn waterfronts as well. Within the past two decades, since the early 1990s, crumbling, decaying, all but forgotten waterfronts have been rediscovered and not only for recreational uses, but for luxury housing, restaurants, sports facilities and marinas. And the likes of fancy corporations are now sometimes housed away from midtown, in restored, revived, converted warehouses and industrial buildings. The Hoboken waterfront – immortalized in the classic 1954 film *On The Waterfront*, starring Marlon Brando – is especially rich in history. It was once thriving with ships and maritime commerce. In preparation, wreckers removed the last of the shipping terminals in the late 1980s.

Some one hundred years ago, in the first decade of the twentieth century, the lower Hoboken piers spaced between First and Fourth streets were the property of two of the greatest ocean liner companies, Germany's Hamburg Amerika Line and North German Lloyd. Well before most of the larger piers that became synonymous with New York City were built, the largest liners yet built (for the Germans) berthed in Hoboken. The Germans had in fact the very first Atlantic superliners, the first of the so-called 'floating palaces'. These ships towered above the tenements of nearby River and Hudson streets and dominated the Hoboken skyline as seen when looking westward from the Manhattan shore.

The greatest day for Hoboken's waterfront and for the Germans might just have been in May 1913. As flags waved, horns honked, whistles screeched and tugs and other craft formed a grand escort, the 919-foot-long, 52,100-ton *Imperator* – a ship immediately dubbed 'the colossus of the Atlantic' – put into the Third Street pier at the end of her maiden voyage from Hamburg and the so-called Channel ports of Southampton and Cherbourg. Her three huge, mustard-coloured stacks and twin, towering masts loomed above the pier sheds, adjacent dock houses and those waterfront tenement buildings. Only the 200-foot-high clock tower of nearby Lackawanna Terminal seemed an equivalent.

But, amidst this gala, high-spirited, proud occasion, it was not the first time that the Hoboken piers had welcomed the largest liner of its time. Sixteen years before, in 1897, the then-new speed queen of the Atlantic, the 14,300-ton *Kaiser Wilhelm der Grosse*, arrived for the first time. She was the first of a new generation of liners, all German at first, and the first to be dubbed 'superliners'. They were also the first 'four-stackers'. Beginning in 1900, they were named *Deutschland*, *Kronprinz Wilhelm*, *Kaiser Wilhelm II* and finally the *Kronprinzessin Cecilie*. Some years later, beginning in 1905, other big, quite noteworthy Germans followed, liners such as the *Amerika*, *Kaiserin Auguste Victoria* and *George Washington*. They were among the finest, grandest and, in ways, also most innovative passenger ships of their day. Along with smaller German vessels, both passenger as well as cargo, the Hoboken docks, all five of them, were often crammed with shipping and all of them flying the colors of the Kaiser's Imperial nation.

That first arrival of the 4,594-passenger *Imperator* was, in fact, the great and grand culmination of this aforementioned group. She was the pride of the great German fleet, the crowning symbol of Teutonic brilliance and technology and engineering. She was not only the biggest liner afloat, surpassing such contemporaries as Britain's speedy *Mauretania*, the immortal *Lusitania*, the innovative *Olympic* and even her otherwise tragic sister *Titanic*, but the new German giant was also the first of three successively larger liners, in fact the very first of the true superliners. The *Imperator* broke just about every record except for Blue Riband-winning speed. Within a year, but in that fateful, peace-shattering summer of 1914, the second of these Hamburg Amerika behemoths, the 54,300-ton, 950-foot-long *Vaterland* had her maiden crossing from Hamburg. She too berthed at the foot of Third Street in Hoboken.

Very sadly, the dramatic untimeliness of the First World War, that 'war to end all wars', changed everything. Among all other Atlantic passenger ships, the third of the Hamburg Amerika Line giants, in fact the largest of all, the 56,500-grt *Bismarck*, never had her six-night maiden crossing to Hoboken. Incomplete, she sat out those war years, quiet and untouched, at a berth at the Blohm & Voss shipyard. And by war's end in 1918, even life for the Hoboken piers would be different. As German-owned and therefore enemy-owned property, it was all seized by the Americans, who entered the hostilities in April 1917. Ships were included in the confiscation and among them was no less than the German national flagship, the 950-foot-long *Vaterland*. In a great and strange irony, those same Hoboken piers were used to send American military forces overseas to fight the armies of the Kaiser. Yankee troops were often ferried on ships now flying the colors of the United States. Often in disguising 'dazzle paint' to ward off the sinister German warships and especially lurking U-boats, their earlier Germanic heritage was masked further – they sailed from the Hoboken piers heavily loaded with troops but mostly under new and far different names as well. The giant *Vaterland* was now the USS *Leviathan*. Other changes included the *Kronprinz Wilhelm* as the USS *Von Steuben*, the *Kaiser Wilhelm II* as the USS *Agamemnon* and the *Kronprinzessin Cecilie* as the USS *Mount Vernon*.

Those first German superliners were in fact inspired by a royal occasion. Kaiser Wilhelm II had attended a British naval fleet review at Spithead in 1889. The Kaiser was intrigued, fascinated, but also deeply jealous. He was very much impressed by the British military craft, but was positively bewitched by White Star Line's *Teutonic*, a 9,000-ton passenger ship that then ranked as the largest afloat. When the Kaiser returned home, it was reported that German shipping was never the same again. Imperial Germany was more prosperous than ever and was on her expansionist path. Shipping was a great priority, and what better way to show off national prowess than on the great North Atlantic route to America. Soon, shipping offices, directors and designers were prompted by the wishes of His Imperial Majesty. With royal blessings and enthusiasm, plans were soon laid for bigger, better, faster ships. Above all else, they must surpass the British, namely those belonging to the dominant Cunard and White Star lines.

It was further decreed that these new German liners must come from German shipyards. They could not be built in, say, the then-great shipbuilding centers of the world in England, Scotland and Northern Ireland. But first, the German shipbuilders needed to learn how to build bigger and better passenger ships. Agents were sent to the likes of Newcastle, Glasgow and Belfast to recruit engineers, designers, craftsmen and highly skilled workers. Their incentives: better wages. In actuality, it was all rather reckless. Soon after the German shipyards learned, copied and then mastered the methods, the British workers were sent packing. By May 1897, just eight years after that fleet review at Spithead, Germany was ready – the 655-foot-long *Kaiser Wilhelm der Grosse* was launched at Stettin.

Capped by only the second set of four funnels (and uniquely grouped in pairs of two) ever to go to sea, the long, sleek *Kaiser* was also almost fearsome-looking. She was to be not only the world's largest liner, but also the world's fastest. On board, she would open up a new era in design and decoration. It was said at the time of her maiden voyage in September 1897 that 'the walls and ceilings of her grand saloons would all but collapse under their own weight'. Later, a witty American writer noted, 'The German liner décor included two of everything but the kitchen range and then gilded.'

Two months after her maiden crossing between Bremerhaven, Southampton, Cherbourg and New York (Hoboken), she captured the prized Blue Riband with a speed of 22.35 knots or a fast crossing of an amazing six days. She also became the first of the so-called 'nine-day boats', sailing between Germany and the United States. Her owners, the North German Lloyd, planned for three larger liners, thereby creating a weekly service in each direction. The Germans, including the be-medaled Kaiser, beamed with pride. And of course they all knew that she was only the beginning. There were bigger and faster German liners already on the design tables. With great popularity from the start, the triple-expansion steam-powered *Kaiser Wilhelm der Grosse* was the first non-British-built speed queen in forty years. Both Cunard and White Star watched with envious eyes as she regularly passed through the Channel. With a fixed glare, one London shipping executive added, 'She has an almost serpent-like tone about her.'

The traveling public was quickly enamored with the new *Kaiser*. There were columned lounges and marble fireplaces, detailed wood carvings and highly detailed stained glass. One passenger wrote, 'It is easy to forget that you are at sea and instead imagine yourself to be housed in some turreted eyrie on the Upper Rhine.' There was one noted blemish to the new liner, however. She was a rather notorious roller and was soon dubbed the 'Rolling Billy'. Westbound immigrants, those souls bound for a new life and opportunity and freedom in the so-called New World and for $6–10 per person per passage, earned her greatest profits, of course. Very quickly, they equated her tall funnels with size, reliability and, most of all, safety. The 'four-stackers' would become the most popular and profitable liners on the Atlantic in those years prior to the First World War. Companies were soon known to add a dummy fourth funnel just for the effect and to lure more of the highly desirable immigrant traffic.

Within two years, in 1899, however, White Star Line countered with the 17,200-ton *Oceanic*, then the largest liner afloat. But soon, Hamburg Amerika Line took its place in the superliner queue with a big ship of their own, the 16,500-ton *Deutschland*, which surpassed the North German Lloyd's *Kaiser Wilhelm der Grosse* by almost 2,000 tons. Grand, ornate, improved and faster still, the *Deutschland* captured the Blue Riband in the winter of 1900. But the glow soon dimmed – she was operationally unsound. Her extremely powerful quadruple-expansion engines caused excessive, passenger-disrupting vibrations, noises and rattling. Her reputation was soon diminished, such that Hamburg Amerika would never again seek the Blue Riband, but instead concentrate on size, luxury and passenger comfort. During 1906 and for a short period thereafter, Hamburg Amerika would again own the world's largest liner, the 24,300-ton *Kaiserin Auguste Victoria*. Later, but far more triumphantly, in 1913–14, they would hold the record with the 52,100-ton *Imperator* and then the 54,200-ton *Vaterland*.

The *Deutschland* was never quite a success or a profitable ship. Within a decade, in 1910–11, she was repainted in tropical all-white and redesigned as the world's first large cruise ship, the *Victoria Luise*. She was restyled with far more comfortable accommodations but for a mere 487 all-first class guests (downgraded from her original transatlantic capacity of 2,050 – 450 first class, 300 second class, 300 third class and 1,000 steerage). She was described as a ship of grand public rooms, elegantly furnished suites and cabins, and considerable amenities such as a gymnasium (with so-called Zander electrical apparatus), electric light baths, shower baths, laundry, photographers' dark room, library, book stall and information bureau.

The Bremen-headquartered North German Lloyd was not to be outdone by Hamburg-based Hamburg Amerika Line and responded with three more superliners, all of them four-stackers, a feature aimed at the highly profitable yet keenly competitive steerage class business to America. The 14,900-ton *Kronprinz Wilhelm* was commissioned in the late summer of 1901 and was followed by the *Kaiser Wilhelm II* in the spring of 1903. The *Kronprinzessin Cecilie* arrived in the summer of 1907. This four-strong team of Lloyd four-stackers were extremely successful, perhaps even more at Hoboken than even at European ports. They were known fondly as the 'Hohenzollerns of Hoboken'. Being the finest and largest in their fleet, North German Lloyd advertised them as 'the fleetest of the fleet'. Their great popularity was based on their regularity – a set timetable of a sailing every week in each direction. They also provided some of the most luxurious quarters then on the Atlantic including large first class suites for $2,000 in 1907. They were appraised in many ways including, 'The interior of these ships, instead of stuffy, uncomfortable prisons, were converted into veritable palaces. A decade ago, it would have been considered absurd to spend money for the interior decoration of steamships. Today the finest hotels in the world do not boast of more gorgeous splendour.' On board the newest, the *Kronprinzessin Cecilie*, décor reached new heights and included a well of daylight that rose four decks and included no less than sixteen isolated columns carrying a new cupola and glass roof. And their service and food in first class were as prized as their décor. There were twenty kinds of warm dishes, besides tea, cocoa, coffee and chocolate, provided for breakfast. Luncheons consisted of, in addition to introductory courses and salads, three or four different soups, a dozen warm dishes, as many kinds of cold dishes, and four or five vegetables. Dinners might run from ten to twelve courses. And an added touch: North German Lloyd introduced the *à la carte* system. As their brochures of the day mentioned, 'No blare of trumpets now announces dinner, for the meal extends several hours, passengers come and go at their will. Meals *à la carte* are served, without additional charge, to those who prefer them. Further, the Lloyd has introduced the small table system – round tables for two, five and seven persons.'

Also known as the 'four flyers', the British were deeply fascinated by, if fiercely envious of, these German four-stackers. A journalist visiting one of the ships at Southampton in 1903 noted, 'It is little less than remarkable that a nation which in the '80s was more or less dependent on this country for the construction of her mail ships should have so rapidly developed her shipbuilding talents that she now produces a vessel which is the largest in the world and which in point of speed promises to equal any steamship yet afloat … and there are features about the *Kaiser Wilhelm II* which represent an approach to luxury in voyaging which has as yet been unattained.'

Above: With her funnels grouped two and two, the great Hamburg Amerika liner *Deutschland*. (Author's Collection)

Far right: A chromo-lithograph poster advertising Hamburg Amerika's *Deutschland*. (J&C McCutcheon Collection)

Right: Scenes taken in dry dock emphasized the speedy lines of the German four-stackers. (J&C McCutcheon Collection)

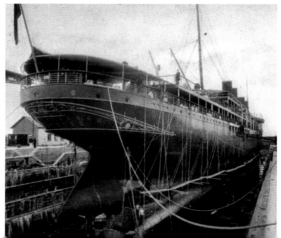

Above: A section of the first class dining room aboard the *Kaiser Wilhelm II*. (Author's Collection)

Left: North German Lloyd's *Kaiser Wilhelm der Grosse*. (J&C McCutcheon Collection)

Right: Rich and ornate: the first class smoking room aboard the *Kronprinz Wilhelm*. (Hapag-Lloyd)

Below right: A postcard view, issued in *c.* 1905, of the *Kronprinz Wilhelm*. (J&C McCutcheon Collection)

Below left: After the First World War, the troublesome former *Deutschland* was demoded with two funnels as the immigrant ship *Hansa*. (Hapag-Lloyd)

Norddeutscher Lloyd, Bremen

BRITAIN'S RECORD-BREAKERS:
LUSITANIA & *MAURETANIA*

It was the beginning of a rather long list of royal and near-royal launchings for the great Cunard Steam-Ship Company Limited, as it was long known. Her Grace the Duchess of Roxburghe did the honors for the launching of the *Mauretania* at Newcastle in September 1906. It was all quite noteworthy and newsworthy. Ocean liners had been proclaimed, after all, 'the greatest moving objects yet made by man'.

The British were not just unhappy, but deeply concerned after the turn of the century with the rising dominance and soaring popularity of the big German four-stackers on the prestigious North Atlantic run. It was not just about Cunard and their position, but also about national pride and prestige and standing. Ministers in London were worried further, even aggravated, when the nation's second-largest liner firm, the White Star Line, was sold to multi-millionaire J. P. Morgan's empire in America. Even if White Star ships would continue to fly the British flag, they were still American-owned. A salvage plan of sorts was devised. The Government turned to the Cunard Line, then having the biggest fleet on the Atlantic, and offered large, liberal loans to build not one but two express liners. They would be the largest ships in the world as well as the fastest, and hefty operating subsidies were included. They were also to represent, especially to the rival Germans and the all-important Americans, the best of British technology, engineering and overall design. In fact, they were to be great symbols of Britain's supremacy in marine propulsion.

The selection of propulsion machinery for these new 'super Cunarders' followed a very interesting and very successful experiment with the then-new steam turbine system aboard another Cunarder, the *Carmania*, commissioned in 1905. The efficiency of the steam turbines aboard that 20,000-ton ship was in fact quite startling. It was, quite clearly, the beginning of the more efficient and powerful steam-turbine-powered ocean liner.

The new twins followed the Cunard naming practice of using Roman geographic locations. The first of the pair, the 31,500-ton *Lusitania*, was named for Roman Portugal; the *Mauretania* took her name from Roman Morocco. They were statistically impressive as well – being some 10,000 tons larger than the largest German four-stacker. They too were given four funnels, which were evenly spaced and, to many, created a finer appearance. Almost everything about them was newsworthy, often mind-boggling. Their funnels, painted in Cunard's orange-red and black, dominated the waterfront at Liverpool and even New York. Below decks, there were twenty-five boilers and 192 furnaces aboard each ship. There was storage capacity for 6,000 tons of coal, which produced a great service speed of 24–25 knots, which meant a consumption of 1,000 tons of coal per day.

The *Lusitania* – which had a capacity for 2,165 passengers – was commissioned in September 1907; the *Mauretania* in the following November. After the quadruple-screw *Lusitania* captured the Blue Riband with the first average speed greater than 25 knots in 1907, her maiden year, Britain very proudly retained Atlantic speed honors for well over two decades. Soon after the *Lusitania*'s triumph, the *Mauretania* made an even faster run, above 26 knots, and eventually established herself as the faster of the pair and holder of the coveted Blue Riband. For this great distinction, lasting for twenty-two years, until 1929, more travelers preferred the *Mauretania*. The British Government and Cunard were especially proud of these speedy sister ships and more specifically of the legendary *Mauretania*, surely one of the most successful and well-liked liners ever to sail.

The interiors of these newest of Cunarders represented the glories of British as well as European design and décor. The decorative themes ranged from French Renaissance to English country, and included grand lounges, elegant smoking rooms, libraries, salons, private parlors and even exceptional Edwardian palm courts. All of the bathroom fixtures in first class were silver plated. And the *Mauretania* had an added feature: the first hydraulically operated barber's chair ever to go to sea.

But if the first class and second class had the greatest comfort, luxuries, even added notations, Cunard made its greatest profits in spartan third class and steerage. As the latest of the 'floating palaces', the *Lusitania* and *Mauretania* were no exceptions. On board the 790-foot-long *Mauretania,* her accommodations were divided between 560 in first class, 475 second class and a huge 1,300 down in third class. Third class was, of course, the greatest profit-making space for her as well as all other Atlantic passenger ships of that time.

Between 1900 and 1915, 12½ million immigrants crossed the Atlantic to the New World. Alone, in 1907, at its peak, there were 1.2 million immigrants and nearly 90 per cent of them made the journey, from six days to as long as three weeks, in third class or steerage. 1 million immigrants came from Britain alone. They lived in crowded, sometimes poorly ventilated, lower deck quarters, often in dormitories. Usually, they were allowed out on the open decks for an hour each day.

At New York, third class and steerage passengers were unloaded from passenger ships that were anchored in the lower reaches of the harbor known as The Narrows. These immigrant passengers were taken by tenders, ferries and even barges to Ellis Island, the US Government inspection station situated just north of the Statue of Liberty. Only the first and second class passengers were permitted to remain and proceed to the Manhattan or Hoboken docks.

In 2001, I prepared the database of passenger ships, 818 in all, that carried immigrants to New York and through the doors and gates of Ellis Island. The project was inspired and underwritten by the Statue of Liberty-Ellis Island Foundation, which has been linked to the former immigration station since it opened as a museum in 1991. Heritage has become very popular, especially with younger Americans, who are often keen to know of their roots and their predecessors who crossed the great Atlantic from the Old World to the New. Their interest often includes the detailing of, say, a great-grandparent's journey and so the ship they crossed aboard. The database therefore includes many recorded ships, from tiny, 1,500-ton vessels that were somehow pressed into immigrant service and often with the most primitive quarters to the likes of major liners such as the *Lusitania*, *Olympic* and *Imperator*.

Today, the museum on Ellis Island is a huge tourist attraction and an exceptionally popular one. More than a third of the people living in the United States today arrived via Ellis Island or had relatives who did. To those earlier immigrants, the actual entry and inspection process was terrifying, even more so than the sometimes harrowing, storm-tossed ocean crossing itself. Ellis Island doctors, for example, were known as the 'six-second specialists', checking immigrants who showed possible symptoms of disease – heavy breathing, limping, coughing, even prematurely thinning hair. If a doctor made a chalk mark on an immigrant's coat, jacket or shirt (such as E for eye), it often indicated need for further medical inspection. For the incoming immigrants, it was yet more fear.

In the second phase of the inspection and interrogation, immigration officials checked information that had already been collected by the steamship firms. In this often tense process, through misunderstandings and the diverse mixture of foreign languages, names were often changed. For example, Fishcov became Fishman. In other documented cases, occupations became last names: Cook, Baker, Miller. Overall, only 20 per cent of all entrants were detained for further examination, and, in the end, only 2 per cent were actually rejected and returned home. For those unfortunate souls, the steamship firms that brought them had to provide return passage. In June 2004, I attended the first Ellis Island Heritage Awards ceremonies. That day, among others, the most famous living immigrant was honored. Unable to attend, however, because of ill health, ninety-nine-year-old Bob Hope had, in 1909, come in third class from England.

Sea life, especially in first class, had its rituals, of course. Passengers loved to sit in large, lavish lounges and especially around fireplaces, which were considered a high point in elegance on the great liners. They were usually entirely artificial, of course, having electrically lighted logs. Great, domed skylights were also a fascination point and flooded lounges and salons with great quantities of daylight. These settings were often on-board refuges from the furies and pounding of huge Atlantic seas, and more especially those ferocious winter storms. Other public rooms, including the writing & card rooms and wood-paneled libraries, were also popular havens of shipboard life. Dining in first class was, of course, often quite exceptional. On board the *Mauretania*, for example, it was a two-deck affair with tables on both levels. One Cunard brochure noted, 'When the ship is in evening dress, the dining room is as gay and brilliant as the Armenonville in Paris or as socially correct as the Berkeley in London.' The dining room on board the *Mauretania* included the captain's table in the middle and a monster arrangement of palms and long-stemmed greens rising up into the balcony area. The center portion under the dome was kept free of tables and used for dancing during the dinner hour.

Crew members aboard the great liners were, in many ways, a unique breed for seamen. For example, to be employed on a Cunard passenger liner was considered prestigious in itself. Often, special contacts were needed just for employment. One captain later recalled, 'The officers in particular were career men, often with over forty or fifty years of service.'

Opposite: The mighty *Mauretania* at Fishguard (an added call before and after Liverpool); the *Mauretania* held the coveted Blue Riband for twenty-two years. (J&C McCutcheon Collection)

Above: Inventor Joseph Swan's invitation to the launch of the *Mauretania* at Newcastle. (J&C McCutcheon Collection)

Above: The *Lusitania* arriving at Cunard's Pier 54 at New York. (Cunard Line)

Above left: The splendid first class main lounge aboard the *Mauretania*. Shoreside décor and style were the inspirations to shipboard design. (Cunard Line)

Above right: The refreshing café aboard the *Lusitania*. (Cunard Line)

WHITE STAR'S TRIO
OLYMPIC, TITANIC & BRITANNIC

On a warm spring evening in 2010, I was guest speaker at the annual convention of the *Titanic* International Society. Several hundred devotees of the tragic White Star liner, horrifically sunk on her maiden voyage no less, and, to some extent, other noted liners, had gathered up in Needham, Massachusetts. Conveniently, Boston is close by. I gave a talk on the great Atlantic liners of the twentieth century. I was hardly an expert on the *Titanic* and her demise and all the details in the aftermath, and so sensibly, I imagined, kept my talk to an overview – from the *Mauretania* through to the modern age of the *Queen Mary 2* and super-mega cruise ships like the $1.5 billion, 6,400-bed *Oasis of the Seas*.

Indeed, we had progressed and grown and, alas, the race for bigger and better was still on. The 882-foot-long *Titanic* was the biggest of her day, in 1912, when in that spring she steamed out of the Harland & Wolff shipyard at Belfast in Northern Ireland. She made course for Southampton, to make preparations for her maiden westbound crossing to New York. All eyes were focused on this newest of the Atlantic's floating palaces. Yes, she was the biggest, at least for the time being, but had a very unique, added cachet: she was said to be the world's first unsinkable ship. Quite simply, she was unique. She was the height of that Industrial Age spirit: bigger, better, yet more notable and distinctive.

In New York City, the skyscraper was another symbol of this age of marveling, Industrial Age distinction. The Singer Building had reached forty-seven floors by the time it was completed in 1906. With a huge American flag waving on top, it was the tallest building in the world. (The 975-foot-tall Eiffel Tower, opened in 1889, was taller, of course, but not a skyscraper, at least not in the same sense.) But the race amidst Manhattan real estate was on: the fifty-two-storey Metropolitan Life Tower followed in 1909 and took the crown as world's tallest. But then the sixty-floor Woolworth Building sprung up, like some sort of springtime flower, four years later. That race for biggest, longest and, of course, fastest also prevailed in shipping company boardrooms and design offices. If Cunard's *Lusitania* and *Mauretania* were the world's largest liners in 1907 at just under 33,000 tons and some 790 feet in length, arch-rival White Star Line, owned by American tycoon J. P. Morgan, but still flying the British colors, could do better – and in doing so, attract more passengers, especially those in top-deck first class. Linking it all to safety, lower-deck emigrants in Spartan steerage might be impressed and then lured as well. White Star planned three ships overall – the first two as a pair, the 882-foot-long *Olympic* and then the *Titanic*. Slightly bigger still, the 48,000-ton *Gigantic* would follow. White Star's place in the hierarchy of Atlantic liner travel seemed assured, well for the time being. (Cunard had their splendid 45,000-ton *Aquitania* on the drawing boards, but far more significantly, the Germans, in the form of the Hamburg Amerika Line, were making their first drawings for a colossal threesome – ships that would become the 52,000-ton *Imperator,* then the 54,000-ton *Vaterland* and, finally, the 56,000-ton *Bismarck.* Indeed, the ocean liner sweepstakes, that grand race, was on!)

Business was booming as the first decade of the twentieth century was drawing to a close. By 1910, with ships growing larger as well as more luxurious, the White Star Line, with no ambition toward great speed or Blue Riband records, decided to concentrate on greater size

and grander accommodations. Their three new liners would be the largest afloat. Internally, they would be the most splendid liners of their day on the Atlantic, each with an Arabian indoor pool (the first ever on an Atlantic liner), first class staterooms decorated in eleven different schemes and a palm court of lush greenery.

The first of the trio, the 45,300-ton *Olympic*, was launched at Harland & Wolff shipyard at Belfast in Northern Ireland on October 20, 1910. But White Star's greatest and perhaps proudest day came six months later, on May 31, when the second big liner, the *Titanic*, was launched at noon. Then, in the afternoon, invited guests, the dignitaries, friends of the line and of course the press, boarded the completed 2,764-passenger *Olympic* for her very first run, an overnight delivery voyage to Southampton. Along with her great size, the innards of the sparkling new *Olympic* were her most attractive feature. To the excited, much-interested press, she was dubbed the greatest yet of the 'floating palaces'. White Star Line was pleased and honored, and looked forward to the second ship, which was even larger, at 46,300 tons. Again, a British-flag liner would be the world's largest and, to many, the most splendid.

As with second sister ships, White Star publicists worked especially hard to find a special identity for the 21-knot, triple-screw *Titanic*. Their efforts were quite thorough – she was already a well-known ship even before her maiden sailing. The company actually went a step further by calling her 'the world's first unsinkable ship'. She had been fitted with extra watertight compartments and, because of White Star's absolute confidence, there were too few lifeboats and insufficient lifesaving gear for her maximum 2,600 passengers and 900 crew.

But the gild on White Star's golden rose began to tarnish and rather quickly. The flag-waving, horn-honking and festive atmosphere of the *Titanic*'s maiden voyage from Southampton via Cherbourg and Queenstown to New York began on April 10, 1912. There were, it seems, some unlucky omens even as the ship set off from British shores. At Southampton, while undocking, she nearly collided with the American liner *New York*. But far greater trouble was ahead. The great tragedy of that westward maiden crossing is extremely well documented – hundreds of books, over 300 poems, seventy-five different songs. It has been the subject of a Broadway musical and Hollywood's first $1 billion mega-film. Fascination with the *Titanic* and her sinking seems unending. Suffice it here to say that, on the night of April 14, she sideswiped an iceberg that ripped a 300-foot-long gash in her starboard side. The cut was fatal, the ship doomed. Two and a half hours later, she sank in a position 380 miles east of Newfoundland and in 12,000 feet of very cold North Atlantic water. An estimated 1,522 passengers and crew perished. Less than two hours later, the first rescue ship appeared, Cunard's little *Carpathia*, and began taking on the 705 survivors (or some 32 per cent of those who had sailed on the *Titanic*).

The tragedy was the worst sea disaster to date and one from which the White Star Line never fully recovered. Safety aboard passenger ships was improved thereafter. To some, the disaster was so shattering, so demoralizing, so dramatic that it was looked upon as the beginning of the end of the British Empire. Dr Jay Wolff, an historian and port lecturer on modern-day cruise ships, gives a very insightful talk on the *Titanic* disaster. 'It was an end to the age of innocence, that age of optimism,' he concludes. 'The sinking of the greatest ship yet built and one that was unsinkable, which in itself was pure and outright defiance, was a great turning point. And it was all cemented just two years later when World War I started and the entire world changed forever. Sadly, we have never regained that innocence, that unbridled optimism, which ended with the sinking of the *Titanic*.'

WHITE STAR LINE R.M.S. "BRITANNIC"—50,000 TONS.
LAUNCHED FEB. 26TH 1914

Above right: The *Olympic* and *Titanic* were White Star Line's first serious rivals to Cunard's *Mauretania* and *Lusitania*. (Author's Collection)

Above left: The boat deck aboard the *Titanic*, scene of tearful farewells. The boats that would have saved those on board were deemed to spoil the open expanse shown here. (J&C McCutcheon Collection)

Left: A company official postcard of the *Britannic*, which never entered service for White Star, instead being converted to a hospital ship and sunk in 1916 without ever carrying a fare-paying transatlantic passenger. (J&C McCutcheon Collection)

THE KAISER'S THREESOME
IMPERATOR, VATERLAND & BISMARCK

In 1990, I was fortunate to have stayed at the Royal Automobile Club in London. That classic structure, that grand institution, evoked the glories of bygone London. It was classic architecture, stately style and, amidst its splendors and comforts, it included a lavish indoor swimming pool. A grand, extravagant creation in marble and Greek columns, it was the creation of brilliant designer Charles Mewès. That same pool, in a similar style, reappeared soon afterward in the great German liners *Imperator, Vaterland* and *Bismarck*.

Years later, in the summer of 1999, during a stop at Liverpool, I had a special outing: north to Lancaster, also in north-west England, and to Heaton Hall Hotel and Restaurant. It had historic interest: the venue contained some of the wood paneling from the Cunard liner *Berengaria*, which in her prior life had been the innovative German flagship *Imperator*. The panels had been extracted from the ship in 1938, before she was scrapped, and then sold at auction. They are, in a small way, a link to one of the greatest of the floating palaces.

By 1910, more than ever, the Germans wanted to surpass the British, and not only for corporate competition but also for national prestige. The Hamburg Amerika Line in particular, under the guidance of shipping genius Albert Ballin, was determined to build bigger and bigger liners. The company planned three successively larger liners and all under the gleaming eye of the Kaiser himself. They selected a three-ship design. Aboard the 52,100-grt *Imperator*, the forward funnel measured 69 feet above the upper deck and ranked as one of the very tallest funnels yet fitted to a passenger ship. (Later, these three funnels would create balance problems and had to be cut down by as much as nine feet.) Two masts towered at each end of the ship. Along her decks were eighty-three lifeboats and two motor launches (figures prompted by the *Titanic* tragedy). She was fitted with four four-bladed propellers that could make 185 revolutions per minute and twin engine rooms that were 69 and 95 feet long and had bunkers for 8,500 tons of coal.

The Kaiser himself launched the new liner at Hamburg in May 1912, and she set off in the following spring on her maiden crossing to America. The public was dazzled by her and her statistics – such as having quarters for as many as 4,594 passengers: 908 in first class, 972 second class, 942 third class and 1,772 steerage. After all, first class traffic on the Atlantic was rising and westbound immigration to the USA was equally promising (nearly 1 million crossed to New York in 1914 alone). Clearly, two even larger sisters were needed.

Some 40,000 people attended the launching of the second, even larger German giant, the 54,300-ton *Vaterland*. She too was built at the renowned Blohm & Voss shipyard at Hamburg and was launched in April 1913. Again, the public was fascinated by her statistics and details. There were 1.5 million rivets used in her construction, the ship's bunkers held up to 9,000 tons of coal and there was space for 12,000 tons of cargo. The 1,180-member crew was headed by a commodore, four assistant captains, seven nautical officers and twenty-nine engineers. And for transatlantic luxury, she was in the top class. The accommodations in first class included a winter garden, social hall, large dining saloon, grill room and smoking room. There was an entire row of shops, a bank, a travel bureau and an indoor pool-gymnasium complex. There were 752 beds in the first class staterooms, headed by a pair of extremely luxurious imperial suites and ten deluxe apartments. In all, the 950-foot-long *Vaterland* could carry up to 3,909 passengers.

Sadly, however, the Germans were not able to enjoy their third giant liner, 'the Big Three' as they became known. Launched in June 1914 as the *Bismarck*, she was the largest of the three at 56,500 tons and 956 feet in length. But weeks later, the First World War started and so the ship sat at her builder's yard, a rusting shell of what was intended to be the world's largest and one of the most luxurious ships. At war's end in 1918–19, the three German giants were in Allied hands as reparations – the *Imperator* to Cunard, to become the *Berengaria;* the *Vaterland* to the United States and soon sailing as the *Leviathan;* and the *Bismarck* completed as the *Majestic* for White Star.

Far left: This hunting motif aboard the German *Imperator* strongly reflected shoreside influences. (Hapag-Lloyd)

Left: Immigrants arrived in New York harbor at the astounding rate of 12,000 per day in 1907. (Hapag-Lloyd)

Above: Immigrant children improvise their entertainment as they cross the North Atlantic. (Hapag-Lloyd)

Right: Immigrants were housed in dormitories, usually separated between women and children and then the men. (Hapag-Lloyd)

Immigrants often selected the ships for their westbound passages by counting the number of funnels, which, they believed, equated safety. Four-funnel ships, such as the *Mauretania*, were said to be safer than two- and three-funnel ships. (Frank O. Braynard Collection)

LAST OF THE ATLANTIC FOUR-STACKERS
AQUITANIA

It was home to some of the greatest liners, even some of the world's largest and fastest. Liverpool was one of the world's biggest and busiest ports. My first visit to Liverpool was in December 1988, on a cold, mostly dark winter's day. I was visiting friends in the north of England at the time. I returned in 1997, but in high summer, a passenger aboard the *Crystal Symphony*, which was tendering from an anchorage in the famed River Mersey. Liverpool was proclaimed Europe's 2008 'City of Culture'. The Queen herself visited that May to help celebrate, all sorts of public events were held throughout the year and many of the world's great Tall Ships, those majestic, heavily masted sailing vessels, had a rendezvous there and then sailed in full review.

Three hours from London by high-speed rail, Liverpool is booming these days, after decades of slow decline, the resulting inevitable decay of a once great seaport and, of course, huge economic transition. The skyline is growing, the old waterfront is being renewed and restored, new museums are being developed and shopping malls and arcades are springing up around the downtown section. There's even a new cruise terminal, opened just last September and with the ribbon-cutting handled by no less than the Queen's cousin, the Duke of Kent. Aptly, the immensely popular *Queen Elizabeth 2* was one of the very first callers.

Maritime Liverpool was once bustling – one of Britain's busiest seaports, together with London and Southampton. Even in the early '60s, with the last of the old colonial Empire still intact, the port was still booming. 'In the late '50s, when I was just fifteen, the City was buzzing. It was just getting over World War II,' remembered locally born and bred Robert Welding. 'The bomb damage was disappearing and there was an air of expectancy.

Of course, the whole City seemed to run on ships and shipping. Alone, there were then hundreds of ships in the British Merchant Navy and tens of thousands of British seamen. The docks in and around Liverpool were crammed. I recall seeing the tall cranes and the vast sheds. There were various tidal basins in and out of the Mersey and miles upon miles of warehouses, some dating back to Georgian days. There was still mostly hand labor in the docks with gangs of dockers. The unions had arrived, however, and so regular wages were in place. And I remember the buses, trains and trams crammed together down at Pierhead, the heart of the waterfront.'

The sights (and sounds) of a great working port such as Liverpool left lasting impressions, creating vivid memories. 'The Overhead Railway [an elevated train system] was still there in the late '50s and you saw all the ships at dock,' added Welding. 'Often, it seemed as if hundreds of ships were at berth. I recall the Landing Stage [a floating terminal] that handled the liners – such as the Cunard and Canadian Pacific passenger ships to Canada, the Elder Dempster ships to Africa, Anchor Line to India and Blue Funnel Line to Australia and the Far East. The other docks were crammed with freighters, flying the house flags of such well-known British companies as Furness Withy, Lamport & Holt, Pacific Steam Navigation, Ellerman, Harrison, Bibby and Federal Steam Navigation. Altogether, it was an amazing sight!

'There were also large fleets of harbor craft, tugboats, ferries and small passenger ships to places such as the Isle of Man,' he added. 'And there was the big shipyard across the River at Birkenhead. The *Windsor Castle*, at 37,000 tons and the largest liner for UK–South Africa service, was built there in 1959–60.'

Robert Welding, now living near Sydney, Australia, revisited Liverpool in 2002. 'It was totally different, so changed, but with great renovation and restoration taking place. The old working port atmosphere is gone, of course. The passenger liners and the cargo ships and even the little steamers are gone as well. But the likes of the twin-topped Royal Liver Building, the old Cunard Building and the Mersey Docks & Harbor Board Building – the famed 'Three Graces' – are still there and so is the Adelphi Hotel, once used by passengers coming and going on the liners. Today, and even if the maritime role of Liverpool has changed considerably, the city itself has greatly improved – socially, economically, educationally, culturally. Today, it is a proud city!'

One of the most palatial liners ever to sail the Atlantic, Cunard's *Aquitania*, called regularly in the early days at Liverpool. Her interiors were described as 'sumptuously Edwardian'. Her Palladian Lounge was painted in red and vellum, and was a design combination of Sir Christopher Wren and Grinling Gibbons. Still under construction when the *Titanic* went down, the 45,600-ton *Aquitania* was the third and largest member of Cunard's three-ship express service between Liverpool and New York. Completed in the spring of 1914, this 901-foot-long ship – said to be the most beautiful of the four-stackers – was barely in service when she was called up for military duties in the First World War. She resumed commercial sailings in 1919, and was appraised as the best of all Cunarders in the 1920s. It was later said that the *Aquitania* had such classical elegance, both inside and out, that she was an inspiration for the design of just about every Cunarder for the next twenty years. The extraordinary *Queen Mary*, commissioned in 1936, was among the ships that were influenced by her design. Again, in the Second World War, she served valiantly, only to be revived for further Atlantic service in the late '40s. By then, of course, she was the last of the four-stackers, a grand relic. In the winter of 1950, the thirty-six-year-old *Aquitania* went to shipbreakers in Scotland. With an exceptional record, she had steamed 3 million miles and made 450 voyages.

unard

1929

Far left: Immigrants used the fabulous posters of the ships, making their selection of which ship to travel on based on the posters of them at village railway stations, pubs and post offices and then counting the number of funnels. (Cunard Line)

Left: Aquitania passing the Calshot light ship, from a 1924 Cunard brochure. (J&C McCutcheon Collection)

Above: In the days before stabilizers, crossings on the Atlantic could be an adventure, sometimes a great adventure. (French Line)

Above right: Wintertime on the Atlantic could be especially ferocious, as seen in this bow view of the *Aquitania*. (Cunard Line)

Above left: The mails gave the fastest liners an added priority. It was the quickest way to get a letter or package from one side of the Atlantic to the other. British liners, such as the *Mauretania* seen here, were designated RMS for Royal Mail Ship. (Cunard Line)

Far right: The 'black gangs' were a very tough group of seamen who lived and worked down in the bowels of the great liners. (Author's Collection)

Right: Coaling the liners, especially the biggest ones, took days, as upwards of 5,000 tons of steam coal were loaded aboard. (Author's Collection)

Far left: At the beginning of the twentieth century, the Industrial Age projected the belief that 'bigger was better'. Here we see the forty-seven-storey Singer Building, completed in New York in 1906, and then the tallest office tower in the world. It was, of course, soon surpassed. The same theory prevailed in steamship line board rooms. (Author's Collection)

Left: The size of the great liners was amplified as seen in this poster of the 901-foot-long *Aquitania*. (Author's Collection)

Above right: The tugboats in posters were often made even smaller so as to emphasize the great size and therefore safety of the Floating Palaces. (Cunard Line)

Above: Grandeur: the stunning main stairwell in the first class dining room aboard the French Line's four-funnel *France* of 1912. (French Line)

Right: The world's mightiest and tallest crane hovers over the world's largest liner, the *Vaterland*, in this view at Hamburg from 1913. (Hapag-Lloyd)

THE WAR TO END ALL WARS
THE LINERS & THE FIRST WORLD WAR

A small monumental stone, the classic commemorative, stands along River Street in Hoboken, New Jersey. Along with the bustling traffic, it once faced the vast and busy docks. They're gone now, however, relics of a bygone era and, in the 1980s, victims of the redevelopers. The stone honors the countless American soldiers off to War, passing through the Hoboken piers in that 'war to end all wars'. One of the great ironies was that the piers and terminal buildings had been German property, owned by the Hamburg Amerika Line and the North German Lloyd. Some of their ships, including the giant *Vaterland,* had been seized after the United States entered the war in April 1917 and were restyled to ferry troops to fight the very nation and people that had created them. Even the Kaiser himself must have found this to be quite ironic. His pride, the 56,000-ton *Vaterland,* was now an Allied troopship, USS *Leviathan.*

Many Atlantic liners stopped sailing abruptly as the First World War erupted in August 1914. Often, schedules were left in chaos, with erratic crossings and some made with a sense of uncertainty and even less than safe conditions. The war was especially cruel, disruptive and even confusing to some of the greatest of the Kaiser's Atlantic liners. The innovative *Kaiser Wilhelm der Grosse* was a very early casualty. Quickly converted by the Imperial Navy in the summer of 1914, just as the war erupted, she became a high-speed armed merchant cruiser. She was ordered to the Atlantic and sank two Allied merchant ships, but faced trouble when her coal supplies ran low. She put into Rio de Oro, a Spanish colony along the West African coast, but soon a British warship opened fire and the two engaged for a short but fierce battle. The German liner was no match and soon the first superliner was sunk and gone forever.

The *Kronprinzessin Cecilie* was eastbound out of New York, on July 29, 1914, when news was received that war was imminent. Quite worrisome – she was not only carrying lots of homeward-bound Germans, but $10 million in gold bars and $1 million in silver, which were bound for the treasuries of Berlin. A safe passage to Bremerhaven seemed impossible and potential capture by the British unavoidable and soon the captain reversed course and sought the safety of a neutral American port. Not everyone on board was pleased, however, and several first class passengers offered to buy the liner on the spot (and for $3 million), raise the US flag and then sail onward to Europe. The captain declined and instead had the funnels repainted in White Star Line colors and thereby disguised, at least at a great distance, the *Kronprinzessin Cecilie* as the *Olympic,* the well-known sister to the *Titanic.* She fled to quiet Bar Harbor in Maine, dropped anchor there and the locals were surprised that the big White Star liner had called unexpectedly. Of course, upon checking with officials at New York, word was flashed that the 'real' *Olympic* was in fact berthed at Pier 61. The German liner's identity was soon uncovered and the vessel soon moved to Boston, where she was later seized to become the USS *Mount Vernon.*

Along with the giant *Vaterland* and a small armada of other German passenger and cargo ships, another four-stacker, the *Kaiser Wilhelm II,* was caught at her Hoboken pier when war in Europe was declared in August 1914. When America entered the war in the spring of 1917, she was restyled as the troopship USS *Agamemnon.* The remaining member of the original 'four flyers,' the *Kronprinz Wilhelm,* was labeled 'the terror of the Southern Seas'. Altogether, she would sink fifteen Allied ships. She had been taken by the German Navy and dispatched to the South Atlantic, cloaked in various shades of disguising gray. Gone were her days as a peaceful, luxuriant express liner. In a sinister redesign, her outer decks now included powerful guns, while within her once magnificent grand saloon was dismantled and converted to a huge coal storage hold. The smoking room underwent similar gutting, but became a vast hospital ward with endless rows of beds and bunks. But after months at sea, her condition deteriorated – there were leaks in the hull, her bow had to be plugged with cement, there was flooding and disease spread amongst her badly strained crew. She eventually fled to the safety of neutral America, to Norfolk, but only to be seized and later repaired and then reactivated as the USS *Von Steuben*.

Mothballed after the war ended in November 1918, only three of these German greyhounds remained by the early 1920s. Idle in Germany during much of the war, the *Victoria Luise*, the former *Deutschland*, was declined as a prize of war in 1919 because of her poor mechanical condition and allowed to remain with the Hamburg Amerika Line. Repaired slowly, she was once again the largest liner under the German flag. She reappeared as the demoded, twin-funnel immigrant ship *Hansa* and returned to the Hamburg–New York run, but her days were numbered. She was sold to local Hamburg scrappers in 1925. Still in American hands, the former *Kronprinzessin Cecilie* and the ex-*Kaiser Wilhelm II* spent the remainder of their days in a tributary of Chesapeake Bay in Maryland. There were dozens of proposals to reactivate them, including as industrial trade fair ships and as refitted, diesel-driven liners on the North Atlantic, but for the United States Lines and in company with the far larger *Leviathan*, the former *Vaterland*. But nothing came to pass, and while the two ships might have been restored for further trooping on charter to the British in 1940, only the scrappers were seriously interested. Both soon finished their days at the hands of shipbreakers at Baltimore. Rusted, long

ignored and mostly forgotten, this was the sad ending for those five once glorious superliners, the first four-stackers, those first 'floating palaces'.

Britain had lost 1,169 ships during the First World War. The most dramatic and publicized loss of the war was, of course, the sinking of Cunard's giant *Lusitania*. Retained and used for commercial service even after the war started, the ship was said to be too fast for the German U-boats and, as a passenger ship, supposedly immune from attack. On all her wartime sailings, some cargo space was reserved for American materials bound for Britain. The official manifest on that fatal sailing, in May 1915, included sheet brass, copper, cheese, beef, barrels of oysters and crates of chicken. But, unofficially, there was a far more ominous cargo: 4,200 cases of small-caliber rifle ammunition, 100 cases of shrapnel shells and eighteen cases of fuses. Some historians contend that the ship also had ten tons of explosives on board as well as 6 million rounds of ammunition and 323 bales of 'raw furs', a volatile type of gun cotton that exploded when brought into contact with water.

While steaming for Liverpool and off Ireland's Old Head of Kinsale, a U-boat fired and struck the *Lusitania* in the bright sunlight of mid-afternoon. It pierced the *Lusitania*'s steel hull under the starboard bridge. A column of steam and water sprayed 160 feet into the air, carrying with it coal, wood and steel splinters. The ship immediately began to flood, taking a 15-degree list from the start. Then there was a second explosion that caused great damage to the bow. Some survivors maintained that this second blast was not the boilers exploding but 'the secret, mysterious cargo' as it was hit with seawater. The *Lusitania* sank eighteen minutes after the first hit.

At the time of the tragedy, the *Lusitania* was carrying 1,959 passengers and crew. She had life-saving gear and lifeboats for 2,605. However, the great list that the ship took almost immediately after the torpedo hit made it impossible to use many of the lifeboats. Furthermore, only six of the ship's forty-eight boats had stayed afloat. As the *Lusitania's* stern section lifted out of the sea, her propellers were still turning and at least two passengers were sucked into the funnels as they dipped below the water and then were shot outward again when a boiler exploded. Some 1,198 perished, of whom 758 were passengers. Of the 159 Americans on board, 124 were lost.

Above, left and right: Call to duty: camouflage was used to disguise the great liners, such as the *Mauretania*, when they were used as valiant troopships in the First World War. (*Left:* Cunard Line. *Right:* J&C McCutcheon Collection)

Above right: Southampton was the main entry port for North Atlantic liners in the 1920s. Here we see the *Leviathan*, *Majestic* and *Berengaria*. The three ships had been seized from the Germans. (Frank O. Braynard Collection)

Above left: Their use as troopships in the First World War proved to governments that the value of passenger ships, especially the large liners, was even greater. (Cunard Line)

Right: Off to Europe: American servicemen set sail for European trenches, often on confiscated German liners. (Frank O. Braynard Collection)

Above left: At over 56,000 tons, the *Majestic* was the world's largest liner in the 1920s and is seen here in the huge floating dock at Southampton. (Frank O. Braynard Collection)

Above right: The indoor Pompeian swimming pool aboard the *Majestic* was a prized amenity. (J&C McCutcheon Collection)

Below left: The gymnasium of the *Homeric* was typical of transatlantic liners of the 1920s. (J&C McCutcheon Collection)

Below right: The *Leviathan*, the largest liner yet under American colors, had been the German *Vaterland*. (United States Lines)

DECORATIVE INNOVATOR
ILE DE FRANCE

There's some connection between the great liners and the great trains. In 1999, I was happily invited on an enthusiasts' excursion from New York to Montreal and back aboard one of those sleek, streamlined, silvery American trains from the 1930s and '40s. It was a grand excursion into the past. At Montreal, we had an added treat: a visit to the shoppers' restaurant atop Eaton's Department Store. It was created for lunches and teas, those rest stops amidst shopping expeditions. Itself done in sleek, streamlined, art deco style, it was said to be inspired by the great ocean liners and, in particular, by the great *Ile de France* of the French Line. She was one of the most significant and important liners of the twentieth century.

The 1920s was a period of some reinvention for the great liners and their owners. There were two great changes, big divides, on the North Atlantic. The US Government started, in 1924, stringent immigration quotas and so the flow of over 1 million in 1914 dropped to a mere 150,000 by the mid-1920s. Shipping lines had to rush to convert austere steerage quarters to even slightly more comfortable quarters in improved third class. Fortunately, a new age of economy-minded American tourists were heading for Europe. Another great change was the mass conversion in the early 1920s from coal to oil propulsion. Passenger ships of all sizes were quickly converted to the new, far more efficient system. Those below-deck stokers, the infamous 'black gangs', were all but eliminated. Along with the immigration quotas, the disappearances of steerage as well as coal-firing were the two most notable and dramatic changes of the decade following the First World War.

Great tourism to Europe did grow, however, in the '20s … there were the superliners, of course, with their magnificent first class quarters, 'Like a Waldorf Astoria that moved,' commented one observer, and their speedy passages between New York and the Channel ports. Southampton, best suited for the big liners, became the busiest passenger port in Britain. Three big liners were needed to maintain a weekly express service to America. Cunard had its 'Big Three' – the *Mauretania*, still the world's fastest passenger ship; the splendid *Aquitania*; and a newcomer, the very popular *Berengaria*, which had been the German *Imperator*. It remains rather interesting that the biggest Cunarder and flagship of the line had German roots. And Cunard did not even overdo renovations to alter or hide her heritage. Arch-rival White Star had the *Olympic* and not one but two German prizes of war, the giant *Majestic*, the intended *Bismarck* and the largest liner afloat in the 1920s, and the *Homeric*, which had been laid down in 1913 (but never completed) as the *Columbus* for the North German Lloyd. The French were back – with the four-funnel *France* and the glorious *Paris*, completed after interruption by the war in 1921. The Dutch had a new flagship in the works, the *Statendam*, but which would also have seemingly endless delays and so not appear until 1929. Deeply wounded and stripped, the Germans were slow to resume, mostly because of Allied restrictions and a shortage of money, but finally created the 32,500-ton *Columbus* in 1924. The Italians, eager to see the Mediterranean–New York route increase in status and popularity, were quite busy as well. In the mid-1920s, they commissioned their largest liners yet, the 32,500-ton sisters *Roma* and *Augustus*. The Mediterranean route now had big floating palaces of its own.

Of course, the biggest and fastest liners had the greatest appeal and, of course, popularity among trans-ocean travelers. In general, the public was fascinated by these 'behemoths' of the sea. At Southampton, it was indeed an added special occasion when one of these ships went into dry dock. Special excursion trains left London's Waterloo Station, often for a fare of less than a shilling. The British public, especially those unlikely to sail aboard the great transatlantic liners, had the opportunity to tour these 'floating cities,' sometimes while they were resting in dry dock, which made them appear larger still. Occasionally, day-trippers were even invited on board for a walk through the vast, fantasy-like public rooms and the 'miles' of corridors. The greatest treat of all was to be invited for afternoon tea in the restaurant.

Unquestionably, the most innovative big liner of the 1920s was the *Ile de France*. In the wake of the 34,500-ton *Paris* built just six years before, a new, sleek decorative style was used aboard the new 43,100-ton liner, which was launched at St Nazaire in 1926. Not especially distinctive on the outside, it was her interiors that proved to be most significant, in fact the 'great divide' for Atlantic liner décor and decoration. The 1,786-passenger ship was the first of the sleek, art deco ocean liners. Immediately praised and highly popular from the start, ocean liners would never again be quite the same. The 791-foot-long *Ile de France* would become one of the most important and significant ships of the twentieth century.

Unquestionably, the *Ile* – as she was often called – was one of the grandest of all Atlantic liners. She typified the term 'high living on the high seas'. While she was not one of the largest or fastest liners, she was one of the very best decorated. She was a ship of splendor, of Aubusson carpets and Lalique lamps, lavish lounges, a main restaurant likened to a Greek temple and a chapel so ornate that it had fourteen pillars. She was, in fact, to introduce art deco to the high seas and, almost immediately, other ships followed in her decorative wake. She was a ship of white pianos and glossy black floors, and was described years later as being 'early Ginger Rogers'. Her staff was prized, hand-picked and often envied – from suave captains to stewards in starched white jackets and those red-suited bellboys in little pillbox hats. It was easy to understand why for some years she carried more first class passengers than any other Atlantic liner.

She had a very full life, in fact, and carried troops to the farthest corners during the Second World War and then, refitted with two instead of the original three funnels, returned to French Line service in 1949. She was retired in late 1958, then sold to Japanese scrap merchants. But there was a last reprieve before meeting the scrappers: she was given a starring role in Hollywood's *The Last Voyage*, during which she was partially sunk in shallow waters.

Above right: It was said that more seagulls followed the French liners than any others because the scraps were better. Here we see the *Paris* from the top decks of her fleetmate, the *Ile de France*. (French Line)

Above left: The main entrance foyer of the *Paris* was a buzz of activity, especially on sailing days – well-dressed passengers, stewards, reporters and small armies of bellboys delivering telegrams, baskets of fruit and great bouquets of bon voyage flowers. (French Line)

Above middle: The twin-level first class dining room aboard the *Paris* which was used some eighty years later as an inspiration for the Britannia Restaurant aboard the *Queen Mary 2*. The two liners were built at the same shipyard at St Nazaire. (French Line)

Right: A first class suite with sitting room in the foreground aboard the *Paris* in the 1920s. (French Line)

'Cunard Line Mauretania, Aquitania, Berengaria (ex Imperator)'

Left: A safe passage was suggested in this 1920s poster of the *Aquitania*. (Cunard Line)

Top: Cunard made much of its trio of superliners. (J&C McCutcheon Collection)

Above: Despite her German heritage as the *Imperator*, the *Berengaria* was the largest liner as well as flagship of the Cunard fleet until the age of the *Queen Mary* in 1936. (Cunard Line)

Right: The *Berengaria* is shown here, as the centerpiece of the superliner trio, with the *Mauretania* to her left and the *Aquitania* to her right, on this Cunard advertising postcard. (J&C McCutcheon Collection)

Below right: Many travelers, especially in first class, preferred the *Majestic* because she was the largest liner afloat. Affectionately, she was dubbed the 'Magic Stick'. (Cunard Line)

Below left: Cunard had a very strong image and the largest passenger ship fleet on the Atlantic in the 1920s. (Cunard Line)

FASTEST OCEAN SERVICE IN THE WORLD

CUNARD

SOUTHAMPTON, CHERBOURG AND NEW YORK

R.M.S. "MAURETANIA"   R.M.S. "BERENGARIA"   R.M.S. "AQUITANIA"

CUNARD LINE

WHITE STAR LINE

THE WORLD'S LARGEST LINER
SOUTHAMPTON

Left: The *Paris* is seen here 'rushing' across the great northern seas. (French Line)

Above: Japanese artist H. Nogami's depiction of the giant *Leviathan* at sea. (Hisashi Noma Collection)

French Line
PIER 57
NORTH RIVER
PIER 90
NORTH RIVER
NEW YORK

LEVIATHAN
UNITED STATES LINES

Above right: The *Leviathan* berths at Southampton's Ocean Dock, *c.* 1925. (J&C McCutcheon Collection)

Below right: Another view of the *Majestic*, but in postcard form. (Author's Collection)

Left: A baggage label, in stylized Art Deco, from the *Leviathan*. (United States Lines)

Top: Traveling between New York and Le Havre was said to be the 'longest gangplank in the world' on board the French Line. (Author's Collection)

Above: Sailing day from New York: the German liner *Columbus* makes her departure, to the great excitement of both passengers and well-wishers. (Hapag-Lloyd)

Below: Crossing the North Atlantic: a top-deck scene aboard the *Columbus*, which sailed between New York, Cherbourg, Southampton and Bremerhaven. (Hapag-Lloyd)

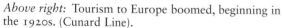

Above right: Tourism to Europe boomed, beginning in the 1920s. (Cunard Line).

Above left: The *Ile de France*, commissioned in 1927, was a revolutionary ship for décor. Afterward, shoreside architects and designers were copying the great liners. It was the beginning of art deco on the high seas! (Author's Collection)

Right: The sleek, art deco style, using lighter woods and fabrics in the furniture, soon became known also as 'ocean liner style'. (French Line)

Left: The first class main lounge aboard the *Ile de France* included a large Aubusson carpet, marble columns and soft, indirect lighting from the ceiling that made ladies especially look 'years younger' with its pink effect. (French Line)

Below left: The first class restaurant on board the *Ile de France* was likened to a modern Greek temple. It included, of course, the *'grande descent'* as an entrance. (French Line)

Below right: A superb painting by Don Stoltenberg of the *Ile de France*. (Don Stoltenberg)

ILE DE FRANCE

NEW GERMAN GREYHOUNDS
BREMEN & *EUROPA*

In March 1977, in the melancholy of that fading, golden afternoon light, a group of ship and harbor enthusiasts floated along the lower end of the Brooklyn waterfront. I was among them and together we were aboard a small boat, the *Pisces*, which was normally in service to the New York City Board of Education. It was a small training vessel for the merchant marine training school. During our excursion around the Lower Bay, the engines were slowed as we paused off Pier 4 of the old, then-long-closed Brooklyn Army Terminal. The 1,800-foot pier, one of three, had been neglected and the effects of the lack of care coupled with weather were most evident: peeling paint, broken windows, the underwater pilings beginning to erode. Its gray coloring had faded as well. In a few years, it would be demolished – gone almost without a trace.

Built just after the First World War, in 1919, the Army Terminal was created especially for military shipping. Soon, however, it was also leased to commercial shipping, particularly as all other harbor piers and terminals were rented. In the late 1920s, the North German Lloyd was preparing for its largest liners yet, the near-sisters *Bremen* and *Europa*. But again, no City piers were available and so the Germans looked to Brooklyn, to the Army Terminal. The lease was soon signed. The *Bremen* and *Europa* would sail from Brooklyn.

Through the ease of post-First World War Allied restrictions, the Germans were allowed to complete the 32,500-ton *Columbus* in 1924. She had been laid down in 1913, but then sat incomplete throughout the war years. She was the largest and finest post-war German liner and her owners, the North German Lloyd, as well as the Hamburg Amerika Line, looked to other new liners, possibly larger ones. Hamburg Amerika had added the 20,800-ton sisters *Albert Ballin* and *Deutschland* in 1923–24, and then the 21,100-ton *Hamburg*

and *New York* in 1926–27. Even more competitive, the Lloyd had, by 1925, planned for two additional 35,000-ton ships, very similar to the *Columbus*. But then, rather suddenly, plans were changed and the planning for this pair of ships was extended to 50,000 tons, larger capacities and, most notably, much more powerful machinery. They were now intended to be the fastest liners on the Atlantic, wresting the Blue Riband from Britain's and Cunard's *Mauretania*.

There had been a very spirited plan to sail two big, 50,000-ton superliners on simultaneous maiden voyages to New York. Together, they would capture the Blue Riband, seize it from the British and the event would symbolize the rebirth of Germany. But unfortunately, on March 26, 1929, the *Europa* – while fitting-out in Hamburg harbor, at the illustrious Blohm & Voss shipyard – caught fire. She was nearly destroyed, close to being declared a complete loss, but shipyard engineers were optimistic. She could be repaired within a year, to be ready for service in the spring of 1930. So, the *Bremen* would be alone and would be first, and sailed to New York on a record-breaking maiden crossing in the summer of 1929. Uniquely for a major liner and Blue Riband champion, she arrived in Brooklyn.

Once in regular service, North German Lloyd publicists were asked to keep these German liners in the news. One way was the addition on the top deck of a Lufthansa seaplane resting in a revolving catapult positioned between the two stacks. This was installed soon after the completion of the two ships. It was a great novelty: approximately forty hours before reaching either New York or Southampton, and if the weather was favorable, the plane would be loaded with priority mail and perhaps even a privileged passenger and then sent ahead. But it was all very costly and cumbersome. For instance, the plane had to be lifted back aboard and replaced in its catapult by a floating crane. By 1935, both the plane and catapult were removed.

Eventually, the Germans lost the speed record to the Italian *Rex*, then to the French *Normandie* and finally to Britain's *Queen Mary*. While Hitler's ministers wanted the *Bremen* and *Europa* to be re-engined so as to regain it, this plan never came to pass. North German Lloyd did plan, however, for the ultimate German-Nazi superliner in the early 1940s. She was to be the 90,000-ton *Amerika*, a projected super ship later renamed *Viktoria*, but then finally abandoned altogether as the Third Reich's wartime advances were reversed.

Above: As built, the *Bremen* and her near-sister, the *Europa*, had flat funnels, which altogether gave them a sleek, almost serpent-like look. The funnels were soon raised in height, however, due to problems with smoke emission.
(Frank O. Braynard Collection)

Far left: Rebirth of the Germans: the *Bremen* is readied for launching in August 1928. She would become the fastest liner on the Atlantic. (Hapag-Lloyd)

Left: A Czechoslovakian advertizing poster of 1937 for the *Bremen*. The German lines advertized heavily in Eastern Europe for passenger trade. (J&C McCutcheon Collection)

Right: A baggage tag from the *Bremen* in the 1930s. (Richard Faber Collection)

Below left: Again, in this artist's view, the ship is made to appear far larger. (Frank O. Braynard Collection)

Below right: A superb art deco poster showing the three North German Lloyd liners, *Columbus, Europa* and *Bremen.* (J&C McCutcheon Collection)

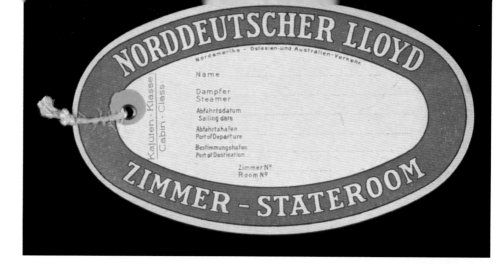

Above right: Another example of fine 1930s design in this close-up rendering of the *Bremen*. (Hapag-Lloyd)

Above left: Proud, mighty and powerful are words that might best describe this artist's depiction of the *Europa*. (Frank O. Braynard Collection)

Right: The fine traditions of German seafarers are exemplified in this poster. (Richard Faber Collection)

Left: The main lounge aboard the *Bremen* was compared to the settings in the classic film *Grand Hotel* of 1933. (Hapag-Lloyd)

NORDDEUTSCHER LLOYD BREM

Participez à nos

macnifiquos croitièra

Top: In 1930, North German Lloyd added a seaplane in a revolving catapult to the top deck of the *Bremen* and *Europa*. One or two passengers and a bag of mail were sent off, beating the ship's arrival by as much as 14 hours. It was actually a cumbersome, even expensive, process, but one that was very pleasing to company publicists. (Frank O. Braynard Collection)

Above: At New York, the *Bremen* and *Europa* were especially noted for their midnight departures with the nighttime City skyline looking like 'diamonds on black velvet'. (Hapag-Lloyd)

Right: At Cherbourg, Le Havre, Southampton and Bremerhaven in particular, there were the aptly named 'boat trains' waiting at the pier-side to shuttle passengers to/from London, Paris and Berlin. (Hapag-Lloyd)

TAKING THE ST LAWRENCE ROUTE
EMPRESS OF BRITAIN

At an auction of ocean liner collectibles, held at New York in March 2010, a painting of the liner *Empress of Britain* sold at a hefty price: $11,000. With three oversized buff funnels balanced on an all-white superstructure and, unusual for an Atlantic liner, on an all-white hull, she looked like the quintessential ocean liner. She was, without question, one of the great 'dreamboats' of the 1930s. In New York, in the early 1930s, the mood was clearly one of 'bigger is better' and so, as the classic symbols of that great metropolis, skyscrapers soared to unparalleled heights. Towers reached to seventy floors. The Chrysler Building, actually topped off in 1929, became the world's tallest at seventy-seven floors and 1,046 feet. But two years later, as the skyscraper race continued, the Empire State Building pulled out all the stops at 102 floors and 1,250 feet. The mood in government ministries and shipping line offices, in Liverpool, Paris and even Rome, seemed to be the same. The theme seemed to be to build bigger, faster, more opulent liners – all of them 'ships of state', great floating national symbols. In particular, it was thought, the Americans would be wowed.

In the wake of the *Bremen* and *Europa*, Great Britain had a momentary spark of notation and increased pride. Liverpool-headquartered Canadian Pacific Steamships added the 42,300-ton *Empress of Britain* in 1931. She was designed to be the largest, most luxurious and fastest liner ever to serve on the Canadian route, using the St Lawrence to and from Quebec City. Another intention was to lure the American Mid-West passenger market. This magnificent, all-white liner – capped by a trio of oversized funnels – was actually dual-purpose: for two-thirds of the year, she would run class-divided Atlantic crossings; for the remainder, she would run four-month cruises around the world out of New York

(minimum fare was $2,000). While her interiors were sumptuous and her amenities included the likes of a complete squash court on the top deck, she was prestigious and notable, but less than economically successful. In the end, Canadian Pacific opted for but one big liner on the Canadian service.

The *Empress of Britain*, seen here transiting the Panama Canal during one of her annual four-month world cruises, was the largest liner built for Canadian transatlantic service. (Canadian Pacific Steamships)

Far right: The *Empress* was capped, as seen in this poster, with three huge, gas tank-like funnels. (Author's Collection)

Right: Canada's Challenger was designed to take some of the Mid-West traffic. (J&C McCutcheon Collection)

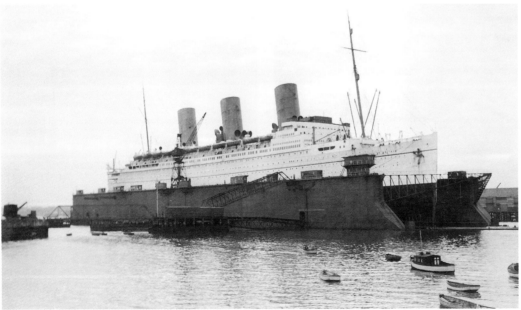

Above right: A superb painting created in 2001 by American artist Don Stoltenberg, showing the *Empress of Britain* and the *Europa* at the Southampton Docks. (Don Stoltenberg Collection)

Above left: Another superb painting by the Japanese artist Hayao Nogami of the *Empress of Britain* at speed. (Hayao Nogami)

Left: The *Empress of Britain* during a pre-world cruise refit in the dry dock in Southampton, *c.* 1933. (J&C McCutcheon Collection)

MUSSOLINI'S DREAMBOATS
REX & *CONTE DI SAVOIA*

Mario Pulice is a dear friend and a world-class ocean liner collector. He specializes in the great French liner *Normandie* and her lavish art deco fittings and furnishings. He has, in fact, one of the very finest collections of that grand ship and it is all housed in his large apartment along Manhattan's upper West Side. But he likes other liners too. One item that obviously caught his eye was a fine model of Mussolini's record-breaking *Rex*. She was the pride of the Italian fleet in the 1930s. He personally restored and repaired the model, and spent hours detailing and enhancing the 4-foot-long model – re-attaching the rigging, repainting parts of it and adding even the smallest details such as the rather tiny multi-colored discs that represented umbrellas along the ship's vast lido deck.

The Italians first entered the 'big ship' leagues in the mid-1920s with a pair of 32,500-tonners, the *Roma* and *Augustus*. They were very successful and prompted Italy's dominant lines on the Atlantic, the Navigazione Generale Italia and Lloyd Sabaudo, to think of larger vessels. In Rome, the Italian Government became interested as well, thinking of the national prestige, and so assured liberal construction as well as operating subsidies. Both the two companies and the ministers in Rome agreed that the new ships must be large, beautifully decorated symbols of Italian design and style, but that at least one of them be capable of wresting the Blue Riband from Germany's *Bremen* and *Europa*.

King Victor Emmanuel III and Queen Elena attended the naming ceremony of the first, larger and more powerful ship, on August 1, 1931. At 880 feet in length, she was named *Rex*, in fact a deliberate effort by the Mussolini regime to further win over royal factions. A year later, in September 1932, and dressed in flags, the 51,000-ton liner set off for America on what was to be a record-breaking maiden voyage. But the fates were against her: off Gibraltar, she had massive engine problems, was delayed and repairs interrupted the westbound sailing by three days. The Italians were mortified. It was a year later, in August 1933, that the 2,358-passenger *Rex* finally captured the Blue Riband with a top speed of nearly 29 knots. She would hold the record until the larger *Normandie*'s arrival in May 1935.

The second of the big Italians was just that – a big ship, but not a speed champ. She was named *Conte di Savoia* at her launching at Trieste in October 1931. But then her maiden crossing, expected to be a gala affair, was marred in troubles and embarrassment. On her first crossing to New York, an outlet valve below the waterline jammed when the 48,500-tonner was just 900 miles east of the North American shore. The jam ripped a serious hole in the hull, which might even have sunk the 814-foot-long liner. Fortunately, the ship's engineers and crew members were resourceful and succeeded in filling the open hole with cement. Carefully, the liner made her way to New York.

The *Conte di Savoia* was the first big liner to have the then-new gyro stabilizer system. She was even advertised as the 'roll-less ship', a niche that publicists and sales personnel much enjoyed. But the concept was oversold. While this gyro system proved successful to some extent, it could not be used, for example, on westbound crossings because prevailing winds might seriously jeopardize the ship's balance and therefore her safety. In reality, passengers aboard the *Conte di Savoia* were often quite surprised to have her rolling and tossing about just like any 'ordinary' Atlantic liner.

In their regular sailings on the so-called 'Sunny Southern Route', between Naples, Genoa, Villefranche, Gibraltar and New York, the *Rex* and the *Conte di Savoia* were great promotional pieces. They were dubbed 'the Rivieras afloat' with outdoor pools, vast open-air deck spaces and striped umbrellas lining a new concept, the lido deck.

Above right: The record-breaking *Rex* departing from Genoa on her maiden voyage in September 1932. (James Sesta Collection)

Below right: It was an Italian Line tradition that the eastbound ship would pass the westbound company vessel. At high speed, it caused something of a sensation for both passengers and crew alike, and was known as the '30 second thrill'. (Everett Viez Collection)

Left: Another of Don Stoltenberg's splendid paintings, this one created in 1997 and highlighting the beautiful *Conte di Savoia*. (Don Stoltenberg Collection)

Above: Don Stoltenberg's oil painting of the *Rex* at sea, created in 2001. (Don Stoltenberg Collection)

Above right: Fanciful advertizing: the bows of the *Rex* and *Conte di Savoia* are seen in this 1932 poster. (Richard Faber Collection)

Right: The magnificent Colonna Lounge aboard the otherwise art deco-styled and -inspired *Conte di Savoia*. (Italian Line)

Left: The first lido decks were created on the Italian liners of the 1920s and '30s, and included this one located between the twin funnels of the *Conte di Savoia*. (Italian Line)

Above right: 'The Riviera Afloat' is emphasized in this stylized depiction of glamorous nights at sea aboard the *Rex* and *Conte di Savoia*. (Italian Line)

Below right: The *Rex* at Genoa. (J&C McCutcheon Collection)

OCEAN LINER EXTRAORDINAIRE
NORMANDIE

On an otherwise rainy winter's night in February 2010, several hundred guests gathered at New York City's South Street Seaport Museum for the gala opening of a special exhibition: 'Decodence: Legendary Interiors & Illustrious Travelers Aboard the SS Normandie'. It was themed to the decorative style of the most stunning of all Atlantic liners, the sumptuous French flagship. No other liner could quite compare to her. She was grand, glorious, record-breaking, innovative, but a true femme fatale – she sailed for only four and a half years. And after a tragic fire and then capsizing, she was sold to shipbreakers in 1946 when she was eleven years old.

'She was, in ways, like a great, incredible, but tragic opera,' commented Mario Pulice, who provided nearly all of the items from the *Normandie* that were exhibited in 'Decodence'. Like Mario, many concede that the 1,029-foot-long *Normandie* was the most magnificent ocean liner of all time. Some say she was also the ultimate in ocean liner design: three huge funnels, uncluttered decks and a perfectly proportioned hull and superstructure. More specifically, she was the ultimate in that great age of art deco ocean liners. She was 'floating Fred Astaire and Ginger Rogers'.

It took over four years to create the brilliant *Normandie*. She was laid down at the Penhoet yard at St Nazaire in January 1931, a month after construction began on her most serious rival, Britain's *Queen Mary*. She was ceremoniously launched in October 1932, but then delayed by the Depression and not completed until the spring of 1935. She immediately attained every superlative – world's largest liner, world's fastest, world's best decorated and, being French, world's best fed. She made the Le Havre–New York passage in a smooth and easy five days. The *Normandie* carried three classes, but is most especially remembered for her sumptuous first class quarters. First class was, as one commentator noted, 'over the top'. The main dining room, for example, was a grand creation of bronze, hammered glass and Lalique. It could seat 1,000 diners at no less than 400 tables. It soared three decks in height and was, as French Line publicists enjoyed noting, longer than the Hall of Mirrors at Versailles. Other notable spaces included the 80-foot-long indoor pool done in tile and with several graduated levels, the first complete theatre ever installed in a passenger ship, the main lounge with its Aubusson carpets and Dupas panels and then the winter garden with live, caged birds and fresh greenery. Every first class stateroom and suite was done in a different décor. These days, on the ocean liner collectibles' market, pieces from the *Normandie* fetch great prices and are second in value only to the *Titanic*. In 1998, a small silver vase from the *Normandie* sold for over $4,000.

Far left: In the early 1930s, bigger was once again seen as better. In New York City, skyscrapers – such as the Cities Service and Bank of Manhattan towers – rose to sixty-six and seventy-two floors. The Chrysler Building soared to seventy-seven floors. (Author's Collection)

Left: The record for skyscrapers went to the Empire State Building, completed in 1931, and which had 102 floors and measured 1,250 feet from street level (and later 1,472 feet with the addition of the TV antenna, added in 1950). Again, liner companies were inspired to build larger liners. (Author's Collection)

Clockwise from right: Interior décor, such as at New York City's Radio City Music Hall, was inspired by the styles of the great liners. It was the age of high art deco. (Author's Collection)

Deco style included the use of large mirrors and stainless handrails and sleek statues. (Author's Collection)

Inspired also by the great liners, the shoppers' restaurant atop Eaton's Department Store in Montreal was said to be based on the *Ile de France*. (Author's Collection)

Hapag-Lloyd handled passenger reservations for the giant German Zeppelins, *Graf Zeppelin* and the *Hindenburg*. Aviation was hardly a threat in the 1930s to the ocean liner business. (Everett Viez Collection)

Left: After sailing aboard the 'floating palaces', dogs were said to never again be the same. Some were said to be spoilt beyond change. (Cunard Line)

Below right: Often regarded as the greatest and grandest of the 'floating palaces', the magnificent, innovative *Normandie* is seen here while under construction at St Nazaire in 1934. (French Line)

Below left: The giant propellers for the record-breaking *Normandie*. (Frank O. Braynard Collection)

Right: After taking the Blue Riband on her maiden westbound crossing, the 1,029-foot-long *Normandie* waits in New York's Lower Bay to begin her final voyage to Pier 88. (Frank O. Braynard Collection)

Below right: Making her way toward her Manhattan berth, the *Normandie* is seen from the air. (Cronican-Arroyo Collection)

Below left: Handsome as well as beautiful from every angle, the *Normandie* had a very advanced appearance. (Vincent Messina Collection)

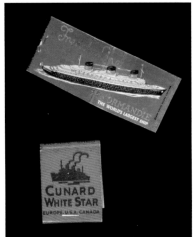

Above: The great ship departing from Pier 88, New York, on her eastbound maiden crossing. (Cronican-Arroyo Collection)

Far left: A magnificent artist's rendering of the glorious *Normandie* at sea, crossing the Atlantic. (French Line)

Left: Matchbook covers from both the *Normandie* and her arch-rival, the *Queen Mary*. (Richard Faber Collection)

RAYMOND-WHITCOMB CRUISE 1939

NORMANDIE TO RIO

Left: In February 1938 and again in February 1939, the *Normandie* made her only cruises: four-week voyages from New York to the Caribbean and Rio de Janeiro for Carnival. Special brochures were issued for these voyages. (Author's Collection)

Right: A somewhat disguised liner, looking like the *Ile de France* as well as the *Normandie*, is made to appear larger in New York's lower Hudson River. She is compared to the hefty, thirty-four-storey Barclay-Vesey Building seen on the left. (Author's Collection)

C.ᵍᵉ TRANSATLANTIQUE
French Line

Havre, Plymouth, New-York

Left: Half of the *Normandie*'s 1,300 crew are assembled on the fore decks in this special publicity photograph. (Frank O. Braynard Collection)

Below left: The foyer in front of the ship's first class restaurant. Flowers are in vases made by Lalique. (Frank O. Braynard Collection)

Below right: Seagoing magnificence: the Grand Salon included Dupas glass panels and furnishings done in tomato red. (Author's Collection)

Above right: The main first class dining room was longer than the Hall of Versailles and was done in bronze, hammered glass and Lalique. There were 275 items on the dinner menus. (French Line)

Above left: Bronze panels depicted the history and glories of France. The ship was not only a floating hotel, but a moving ambassador for French culture, design and décor. (French Line)

Right: The winter garden, with caged birds and live greenery, was an especially popular refuge for first class passengers on dark, gray winter crossings. (French Line)

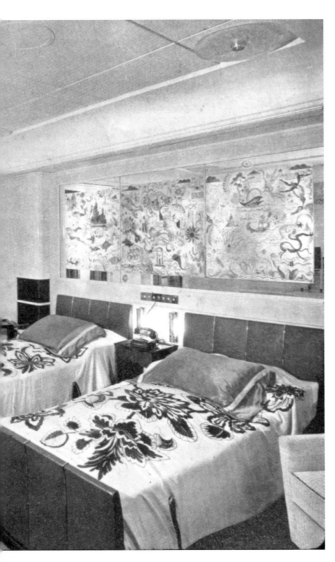

Above right: A portion of the sumptuous Deauville Penthouse aboard the *Normandie*. Sleeping up to eight, it was priced from $2,000 for a five-night passage in the late 1930s. (Frank O. Braynard Collection)

Below right: The indoor pool was eighty feet of tiled, graduated levels. (French Line)

Left: The bedroom of one of the ship's array of ultra-luxurious penthouses and suites. (French Line)

Right: The chapel sat 150 at one time and included a complete altar and Stations of the Cross. (Frank O. Braynard Collection)

Below right: The ship's playroom in first class included a small theatre. (Frank O. Braynard Collection)

Below left: The *Normandie* was, however, a fragile ship and an easy 'roller' as seen in this view from the starboard bridge wing. (Frank O. Braynard Collection)

Outbound and passing the Lower Manhattan skyline, the *Normandie* sets off on her eastbound maiden crossing. (James Sesta Collection)

BRITAIN'S CHAMPIONS
QUEEN MARY & QUEEN ELIZABETH

On a flawless Sunday afternoon in October 2008, I climbed to the top of the last remaining hammerhead crane at what had been the John Brown shipyard at Clydebank in Scotland. A flawless day, the view was expansive – the great River Clyde and the shoreside surrounding it created a beautiful tapestry. It was a quiet Sunday afternoon and so possibly more reflective. Just below had been the docks and slipways where, among almost countless other liners, the *Lusitania*, the *Empress of Britain* and, ever-immortal, the *Queen Mary* and *Queen Elizabeth* had been built. The last big liner to come out of John Brown's was the *Queen Elizabeth 2* in the late 1960s. By the 1990s, the yard had been closed and all but dismantled completely.

The early 1930s could not have been a worse time for shipping. The North Atlantic grew short of its most precious commodity – passengers. The sinister Depression was felt worldwide. Passenger liners began to sail half-full, and sometimes close to empty, and occasionally scarred with rust streaks, the result of deferred, costly maintenance. Even the great Cunard Line and its once booming rival White Star soon found that they had too many ships. The directors of both companies were worried, however, that the express services of both companies were run by aging superliners. The grand *Mauretania* was twenty-three years old by 1930, for example. To complicate matters, Continental firms were making significant strides. The French had added the stunning *Ile de France* in 1927 and planned three more liners, including the ultra-luxurious *Normandie*; the Germans had added two greyhounds, the *Bremen* and *Europa*; and even 'those distant Italians' had twin super ships on the drawing boards, the *Rex* and *Conte di Savoia*. Britain needed to regain her prominent position, her retaliation to the competition.

Despite its increasing financial ills, in June 1928 White Star ordered its biggest liner yet, the 60,000-ton *Oceanic*. She was intended to break records, including the first liner to exceed 1,000 feet in length. She would cost a hefty £3.5 million. Simultaneously, Cunard designers planned an even bigger ship, a projected 75,000-tonner (actually completed in excess of 81,000 tons), the illustriously immortal *Queen Mary*. Inevitably, the two ships would have been teamed.

But the *Oceanic* was never to be. Within thirteen months of the start of her construction at Belfast, the increasingly fragile White Star Company was forced to cancel the order and the small skeleton was cut up, making way for a more moderate liner, the 27,000-ton *Britannic*. But worse times were ahead. White Star posted losses of nearly £500,000 and all while passenger lists dropped by nearly a quarter of a million by late 1931. For Cunard, the British Government came to the rescue. In 1933, a loan of some £9.5 million was authorized – divided as £3 million to complete the *Queen Mary* (then enduring a near two-year delay at Clydebank), £5 million toward a running mate, also for Cunard (the *Queen Elizabeth* of 1940), and £1.5 million of working capital, provided Cunard and White Star merged. And so, on January 1, 1934, Cunard-White Star Limited was formed. In this marriage of rivals, Cunard – with fifteen liners of its own – acquired another ten passenger ships, including what was then the largest in the world, the 56,500-ton *Majestic*. But, as the Depression lingered and as the Atlantic trade barely improved, disposals – most of them from White Star – became the order of the day. Ships such as the *Olympic* and *Homeric* found their way to scrapyards while the mighty *Majestic* had a spark of life as a moored training ship for the British Admiralty at Rosyth, in Scotland.

Two of the three greatest Atlantic liners ever built were the *Queen Mary* and her slightly larger companion ship, the *Queen Elizabeth* (the third of this grand trio was, of course, the French *Normandie*). While the *Queen Mary* laid claim to being the world's fastest liner, the *Queen Elizabeth* was the world's largest of her day. There have been endless books written, for example, on the Cunard *Queens*. Their success was brilliant, their contributions in both peacetime and war were invaluable and their reputations magical. The *Queen Mary* was always the slightly more beloved. At construction, she was to have been named *Victoria*, with the traditional 'ia' ending of nearly all Cunard steamships. When the time came to inform King George V of this decision, Sir Percy Bates and Sir Ashley Sparks, two of the top people at Cunard, requested an audience at Buckingham Palace. It was left to Sir Ashley, who was Cunard's top representative in North America, to speak to the King. He said, 'Your Majesty, we are pleased to inform you that Cunard wishes your approval to name our newest and greatest liner after England's greatest queen.' Without a moment's hesitation, the King replied: 'My wife would be delighted.' His wife was Queen Mary and that was that! This account was given to the late maritime author Frank Braynard in 1946 by Vincent Demo, Cunard's co-chairman in North America. Frank then told the story in his first book, published in 1947 as *Lives of the Liners*.

The King watched as the Queen named the giant liner at the John Brown yard at Clydebank on September 26, 1934. Tens of thousands cheered and waved as the great ship, 1,018 feet in length, went down the ways. She was the pride of Britain, the great flagship of the entire merchant navy and, according to *Planet News*, 'the greatest ship ever built'. On June 1, 1936, to a tremendous reception of tugs and tooting horns and overhead planes, she reached New York for the first time. She was soon proclaimed the fastest liner afloat, holder of the coveted Blue Riband, with her best record being 31½ knots. She was also an instant success, with an average occupancy factor in her first years of 98 per cent (compared to, say, the 59 per cent of the rival *Normandie*). The *Queen Mary* would sail for thirty-one years, becoming one of the most successful superliners of all time.

Even larger, the 83,673-ton *Queen Elizabeth* was due to come into service in April 1940, creating the very first two-ship express service on the Atlantic. But the dramatic eruption of war in Europe in September 1939 changed all that. More contemporary in overall design with, for example, two funnels rather than three as on the *Mary*, the *Queen Elizabeth* was launched on September 27, 1938. She was named by Queen Elizabeth (later the Queen Mother), who was accompanied by her two daughters, Princess Elizabeth and Princess Margaret. Coincidentally, in a little less than thirty years, in September 1967, Princess Elizabeth, as queen, would return to the same Clydebank shipyard to christen the successor, the *Queen Elizabeth 2*.

While waiting at her shipyard berth at Clydebank in the threatening fall and winter of 1939–40, the incomplete, 1,031-foot-long ship was ordered away, to the safety of North American waters and far away from Hitler's sinister bombers. Painted in all-gray and so looking quite somber, the brand-new but incomplete *Elizabeth* reached New York on March 7, 1940. Within months, the *Mary* and the *Elizabeth* were both busily in Allied war duties, working to become the most important and valuable troopships of all time.

While the 1930s was a great era for superliners, the continuation of the age of the floating palaces, it was also a high-water period of medium-sized Atlantic liners. The French, for example, added the *Lafayette* and *Champlain*, the Americans launched the *Washington* and *Manhattan*, and Britain delivered the *Britannic* and *Georgic*. Later, new flagships would be built for the Netherlands, Poland, Sweden and Norway too.

Above: King George V accompanied the Queen during the highly publicized, well-attended launch ceremony at the John Brown Shipyard. (Cunard Line)

Left: While the name *Victoria* was considered first, Her Majesty Queen Mary gave her name to the new Cunard superliner at the Clydebank launching in September 1934. (Frank O. Braynard Collection)

Above left: It took four tons of soap and grease to lubricate the slipways as the 1,018-foot-long *Queen Mary* was launched. (Cunard Line)

Left: There were 600 clocks on board the new *Queen Mary* as well as 4 million rivets, fifty-six kinds of wood from throughout the vast British Empire and, as fascinating distinctions for the public, a rudder so large that two men could go inside. (Cunard Line)

Above: Royal procession: the stately *Queen Mary* arrives in New York for the very first time, in June 1936, surrounded by a flotilla of harbor craft. (Cronican-Arroyo Collection)

THE DEPRESSION
HARD TIMES ON THE HIGH SEAS

In October 2008, during the so-called 'Farewell to the British Isles' cruise aboard the *Queen Elizabeth 2*, I visited Newcastle for the very first time. A great city and seaport in itself, I opted for an excursion to Alnwick, especially to visit the White Swan Hotel. The purpose: to see the wood paneling from the grand old *Olympic*, sister ship to the immortal *Titanic*. It had been purchased in the mid-1930s, in the continuing, hard-pressed years of the Depression, when the ship was being dismantled at nearby Jarrow. Monies were short and much needed, and even the sales of the ship's polished woods were significant. In 2008, over seventy years later, they still looked superb.

Like the *Olympic*, many Atlantic liners, including some of the largest, went to the breakers in the hard-pressed 1930s. Perhaps the saddest was the case of a smaller Atlantic liner, the 22,000-ton *Minnetonka* of the Atlantic Transport Line. She was commissioned in 1924 for London–New York service, but was laid up, due to the Depression, after little more than nine years. Idle for a year, she was unable to find a buyer and so was sold for scrap in 1934. The 626-foot-long ship was just ten years old. My grandfather, a forty-year veteran of the Hoboken police force, often recalled the liner *Leviathan*, mothballed and rusting in the mid-1930s. She was moored at the foot of 2nd Street, in fact at the old German liner piers where she had berthed in earlier, better days as the German flagship *Vaterland*. Now, her days were over. She was a victim of the Depression – and, more specifically, of too few passengers and high operational costs under the American flag.

On the struggling North Atlantic of the 1930s, many steamship owners sent their ships, even the largest Atlantic liners, on alternative cruises to the tropics. These voyages, often less expensively priced, were very popular and earned added revenues for otherwise less than half-empty company accounts. Cruises were voyages of pure relaxation, without a distinct destination as the goal. The North Atlantic passage often had, after all, inclement weather – gray, overcast skies; rains and strong winds; sometimes sinister fogs. In winter, storms could be ferocious – full-scale blizzards and treacherous seas. But on tropical cruises, the voyage was often tranquil, sometimes like sailing on a 'sheet of glass', from start to finish. The most popular cruises from New York were three to seven days in length and sometimes up to two and three weeks around a dozen Caribbean islands. There were $15 overnight cruises aboard the *Olympic*, five days to Nassau for $60 on the *Empress of Britain* and $125 for two weeks around the Caribbean on the *Britannic*. But there were also long cruises, and some much longer. Cunard's 20,200-ton *Carinthia* and *Franconia* often made annual circumnavigations of the globe – 38,000 miles in all, 150 days of cruising, visiting fifty-one ports in twenty-one countries and colonies. The ships were advertized as being among the finest Cunarders of their day – with unique equipment, instantaneous running hot water in every room used, beds six inches wider than on other ships, exceptional deck space, and a squash court and pool.

By direction of SIR JOHN JARVIS, Bt., M.P.

PALMER'S YARD, JARROW
NEWCASTLE-ON-TYNE

CATALOGUE OF
THE COSTLY APPOINTMENTS
FURNISHINGS AND PANELLING
OF

R.M.S. BERENGARIA
(ex "IMPERATOR" and 52,000 Ton Cunard-White Star Liner)

Numerous Sets of Louis XV and 17th and 18th century design CHAIRS : luxurious
LOUNGE CHAIRS and SETTEES : UPRIGHT PIANOFORTES : WILTON and
AXMINSTER CARPETS : the fine PANELLING of the Principal Saloons and Cabins :
and the APPOINTMENTS and FURNITURE of the Cabins throughout : TABLE-
WARE : ELECTRIC LIGHT FITTINGS : SANITARY FITTINGS : HAIR-
DRESSERS' CHAIRS and EQUIPMENT : SHIP'S BELLS : LIFEBOATS : DECK
GEAR, and other Miscellaneous Effects.

WHICH WILL BE SOLD BY AUCTION BY

HAMPTON & SONS
IN CONJUNCTION WITH
ANDERSON & GARLAND
ABOARD THE SHIP, IN PALMER'S YARD, JARROW
On MONDAY, JANUARY 16th, 1939,
AND NINE FOLLOWING DAYS
(JANUARY 16th—20th, and JANUARY 23rd—27th inclusive)
AT 11 O'CLOCK EACH DAY.

General View (Admission by Catalogue only, price 2/6), THURSDAY, FRIDAY,
and SATURDAY, JANUARY 12th, 13th, and 14th, from 10 a.m. to 4 p.m. each day.

Catalogues from the Auctioneers :

HAMPTON & SONS, LTD., 6 Arlington Street, LONDON, S.W.1.
Telephone : Regent 8222 (13 Lines). Telegrams : "Selanet, Piccy, London."
ANDERSON & GARLAND, Newmarket Street, NEWCASTLE-UPON-TYNE, 1.
Telephone : Newcastle 26278.

Or from :—THE JARROW SHIPBREAKING CO., JARROW.

Above left: End of the line: the twenty-eight-year-old *Mauretania* is seen being broken up at Rosyth later in 1935. The first breed of 'floating palaces' were disappearing all too quickly in those lean Depression years. (Frank O. Braynard Collection)

Above middle: The fixtures and fittings aboard the ships were sold off at huge week and ten-day-long auctions. The ship's bridge bell of the *Berengaria* sold for 21 guineas and a lifeboat could be had for £9 9s (approximately $38). (J&C McCutcheon Collection)

Above right: The *Olympic*, which had shared a berth in Southampton's Western Docks with the *Mauretania*, also sailed for breaking, this time to Jarrow, and is shown here on the Tyne in 1935. (J&C McCutcheon Collection)

Left: 1935 was a sad year for the ocean liner, with two famous vessels meeting their ends. The *Mauretania* went first and is shown here at Rosyth on 14 July 1935. (J&C McCutcheon Collection)

Right: Steamship line publicists began to promote the celebrities, royalty, politicians, but mostly the Hollywood stars, who sailed on the great liners. Here we see Fred Astaire aboard the *Queen Mary* in 1938. (Cunard Line)

Far right: Marlene Dietrich departing for Europe with thirty-eight trunks in 1937, on board the *Normandie.* (French Line)

Left: Actor Robert Taylor aboard the *Queen Mary* in 1939. (Cunard Line)

Far left: New York's 'Luxury Liner Row' in February 1939: (from top to bottom) the *Conte di Savoia, Aquitania, Georgic, Normandie, De Grasse, Columbus, Bremen* and *Hamburg.* (James Sesta Collection)

ANOTHER BATTLE: CARRYING THE TROOPS IN THE SECOND WORLD WAR

The lights of Europe went out, quite abruptly, on September 1, 1939 when brutal Nazi forces invaded neighboring but innocent Poland. On September 3, Britain and most of Europe was at war and, once again, ocean liners felt the harsh effects. Most commercial sailings were soon stopped – the seas were no longer quite safe. U-boats lurked in the North Atlantic, sinking their first unarmed liner on the day war started, the *Athenia* of Donaldson Line going down with the loss of 117 passengers and crew.

Often, I meet interested fellow passengers aboard contemporary voyages. Ninety-year-old Rudy was friendly and personable, and told me he had a white Rolls-Royce at home. That luxurious auto is, as I think I can guess, a great symbol of his success in America. He was not an overly pretentious man, but charming, kind, humorous and a great example of living life to the fullest at a very great age. He had a certain zest and reminded me of the late Billy Wilder, also German-accented and of course a very famous Hollywood director. Rudy was traveling with his 'bride', Trudy, who was eighty-nine. Both lost their respective partners after sixty-year marriages and then, happily, had found one another.

Rudy almost never reached America. Being Jewish, he 'escaped' from Germany, sailing on the liner *Bremen*, in March 1939, for New York. Months later, in September, the Second World War started in Europe and such a voyage, such an escape, would not have been possible. Even the *Bremen* stopped sailing, having made her own escape from New York (without passengers, but simply 900 loyal, saluting, arms-outstretched crewmembers), and on a very long, secretive voyage that saw the pride of Hitler's merchant marine being painted in disguising grays while at sea, going far north up to Murmansk and then clinging in and out of fog banks close to the Norwegian coast (so as to avoid the British warships that wanted to capture or even sink the ship) before making it to the safety of her homeport waters.

But a day after Rudy and his family departed from the Bremerhaven docks and the ship steamed west for the New World and freedom, there was news that Germany might be calling up all available men to help 'their friend Mussolini' in his conquest of Ethiopia. Rudy was, of course, eligible, but only as a slave laborer since Jews could not serve in the German military at that time. At nineteen, he was very frightened. The *Bremen* was, after all, German territory until she reached the confines of New York harbor six days later. Rudy could be conscripted and sent back on the return voyage. But Rudy made friends (and exchanged some money) with a cook in the ship's galley. He took refuge, especially from the Nazi agents on board and also from the mostly loyalist crew, and hid in a cold storage locker. He did not appear again on the open decks, in the lounges or in his cabin. He succeeded, quite fortunately. But he did finally appear on an aft, lower deck as the *Bremen* entered New York's Lower Bay and, rather expectedly, cried at the sight of the Statue of Liberty. But he was weak, tired, hungry and very pale from his days in that locker in the galley. He was given whisky by a crewmember to at least add 'some color' to his pale cheeks, but soon became somewhat light-headed, even slightly drunk. So, during immigration at the West 46th Street pier, Rudy was almost suspicious enough to be questioned extensively, even interned. He might even have been sent back to Germany. It all passed and a German-accented young man was waiting behind the pier barricade to greet him. He was, of course, still frightened, fearful of some extended plan to get him back to Germany. He was intimidated by New York City, its vastness, the canyon-like tall buildings and the pure 'electricity' of so many people rushing about. Rudy had come, after all, from a small German village. He was, as he told me, frightened most of all by the black taxi driver. Having never seen a black person, the driver might just as well have been a Martian.

Rudy was taken to an apartment on the upper west side of Manhattan, only to find that it was occupied by his grandfather's best friend from fifty years before. Finally, he was at ease, made to feel comfortable. Typically, he saw America of the 1940s as a great refuge, his escape from death and, quite typically, began to make his way, forge his mark. He went on to form a light transport business and invented several specialized variations of freight carts and wagons, which he sold to none other than the US Post Office and later to Federal Express. Expectedly, he made millions.

On an otherwise quiet Sunday morning, September 3, 1939, Prime Minister Neville Chamberlain broadcast by radio to 47 million Britons that the country was at war with Germany. Worried families huddled around the likes of brown-enamel wireless sets. 'Everything seemed to change,' remembered the late Bernard Erskine, who lived near Southampton. 'The *Queen Mary* had already fled to the safety of America and other liner services came quickly, almost abruptly to a halt. Some ships were already painted over in wartime gray and the docks, always open to the public, were now strictly off limits. We were at war and strict secrecy prevailed. Soon, great liners such as the *Arandora Star*, the *Empress of Britain* and the *Viceroy of India* would be lost.'

Most tragically, the 42,300-ton *Empress of Britain* would not only be among the first losses of the war, but the biggest Allied ship to be lost as well. She was being used as a troopship when, on October 26, 1940, she was attacked by Nazi bombers when a mere seventy miles north-west of the Irish coast. Fortunately, all but forty-nine of her 600 passengers and crew were saved. The blistered and scarred hull of the one-time queen of the Canadian Pacific fleet was under tow by a Polish destroyer. Two days later, however, a Nazi U-boat sighted the blistering liner and fired two torpedoes. They hit their mark and the 758-foot-long *Empress* sank quickly.

Both the *Bremen* and *Europa* were idle in the war. Plans to rebuild them as aircraft carriers or even use them as large troop carriers never came to pass. The *Bremen* was the more unfortunate, however. On March 16, 1941, a young crewman, unhappy with the Nazi regime, set her afire. She later capsized. Later, her remains were cut up for the Nazi war effort and then the very last pieces were taken to a lower part of the River Weser and deliberately sunk. Although neglected and rusting, the *Europa* fared better and was seized at Bremerhaven by the invading American forces in May 1945. Reactivated as the trooper USS *Europa*, she was plagued with fires and soon given to the French as reparations (for the *Normandie)* and then, after extensive repairs and refitting and restyling, re-emerged as the *Liberte*, flagship of the French Line, in 1950. She sailed in Atlantic service until scrapped in 1962.

The splendid *Normandie* was another casualty, after having a very short career. In August 1939, as war clouds were forming over Europe, she was abruptly laid up at New York's Pier 88. For the next two and a half years, she sat: waiting, silent, looked after by a maintenance crew of 100. There were rumors that the US Government would make her over as a large aircraft carrier, but following the attack on Pearl Harbor on December 7, 1941, she was seized by the Americans, who were now officially at war, and underwent an immediate conversion to a 15,000-capacity troopship. Those lavish fittings were soon sent ashore for wartime storage. The ship was soon renamed USS *Lafayette*. But haste and carelessness ensued and, with transformation work well underway at her West 48th Street berth, sparks from a welder's torch ignited a fire that soon spread throughout the ship. The great *Normandie* burned on the cold afternoon of February 9, 1942. The blaze was horrifically destructive, but it was the actual firefighting that spelled her end. Deep in the bitter cold of night, she became so overloaded with water that she listed and finally capsized, resting on her port side in the ice-filled Hudson River. The next morning, canted over and looking like a big, dead whale, she was resting in the mud. Later pumped out and righted (in a huge process that cost $5 million), she was cut down and her scarred hull laid up until it was declared surplus after the war was over, in 1946. Local Port Newark, New Jersey, scrappers bought her remains for a mere $161,000. Indeed, it was a tragic ending, much like an opera.

The big Italian liners were laid up once Mussolini and his regime entered the war in Europe in the late spring of 1940. Tragically, neither the *Rex* nor the *Conte di Savoia* would ever sail again. For security reasons, the *Rex* was laid up along the Adriatic coast, at Bari, but later was moved to a quiet mooring near Trieste. There had been rumors that she would be converted to a giant aircraft carrier, but that never came about. Then, there were reports that the occupying Nazi forces would sink her as a giant blockade to Venice. Instead, on September 8, 1944, the partially disguised liner was sighted by Royal Air Force bombers and was hit with no less than 123 rockets. That great but empty ship burst into flames from end to end, a total ruin. She soon rolled over and sank in shallow waters off the coast. Scrapping began several years later, in 1947, and was not completed until as late as 1958. The *Conte di Savoia* was also laid up, but near Venice. On September 11, 1943, the Nazis ordered that the idle ship, which might fall into Allied hands, be set afire. She burnt out completely and was left as a scorched shell. She was salvaged soon after the war ended, in October 1945, but was of no further use and then her remains were demolished in 1950.

The Second World War was also a period of great heroics, some played by the floating palaces. Hundreds of passenger ships served as troopships, armed cruisers, hospital ships, floating communications centers and even floating repair ships. It was an incredible, urgent, pressing period. But greatest honors must go to the *Queen Mary* and *Queen Elizabeth*. They were the most successful troopships of the Second World War. At first, they operated across the Indian Ocean with troops from Australia for the North African campaigns, returning with the wounded, evacuees and prisoners of war. The *Mary* resumed sailing on the North Atlantic in early 1942 and began something of a military shuttle between New York and Gourock in Scotland. She averaged 15,000 military personnel per crossing (compared to her peacetime capacity of 2,139). Due to her great speed, which was beyond any escort craft, she sailed alone: dark, radio silent and often zigzagging. Aptly, she was dubbed the 'Grey Ghost'. One serious incident did tarnish her otherwise sterling record, however. On October 2, 1942, going at top speed off the Irish coast, she rammed and sliced in two HMS *Curacoa*, a British escort cruiser. The warship sank within three minutes, and all but twenty-six of her 364 crew members were lost. Because of the high danger of possible undetected U-boats, the *Mary* could not stop to rescue any survivors and was forced to continue at full speed.

The *Queen Elizabeth* joined the transatlantic military relay in 1943, and for the next two years the two big Cunarders ferried hundreds of thousands of service personnel. The *Mary* actually established the all-time record for any ship when she left New York in July 1943 with 16,683 aboard. Quite rightly, Winston Churchill later proclaimed that the two *Queens* helped to shorten the war in Europe by at least a year.

At the war's end, by the summer of 1945, a third of the world's passenger ship fleet had been destroyed. This included some of the largest and grandest of Atlantic liners. But one might wonder if, say, had the *Normandie* survived would she have returned to service and, if so, with what modifications, upgrades and redecorations.

Above: Prepared for any emergency! On September 9, 1939, Cunard's *Carinthia* sailed for Britain, her hull camouflaged, her bridge sand-bagged and her passengers prepared. Three British ladies are shown at New York, with their lifebelts on. (J&C McCutcheon Collection)

Left: The *Normandie* seen in better, more peaceful times – but on September 1, 1939, the lights of Europe went out when the Nazis attacked and invaded innocent Poland. Another world war was days away. (Frank O. Braynard Collection)

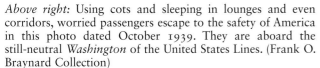

Above right: Using cots and sleeping in lounges and even corridors, worried passengers escape to the safety of America in this photo dated October 1939. They are aboard the still-neutral *Washington* of the United States Lines. (Frank O. Braynard Collection)

Right: The safety of New York: passengers line the decks of an inbound liner in this poetic scene from the fall of 1939. (Frank O. Braynard Collection)

Above: Arturo Toscanini made it to the safe shores of America in October 1939. (Frank O. Braynard Collection)

Above right: As seen from a hammerhead crane at the John Brown shipyard, the second big Cunarder, the 1,031-foot-long *Queen Elizabeth*, is ready for her royal naming and launching in this view from September 1938. (Frank O. Braynard Collection)

Above left: Quickly repainted in wartime gray, the *Queen Mary* waits at New York in this scene from September 1939. The *Aquitania* is to the right; the bow of the *Normandie* on the far left. (Frank O. Braynard Collection)

Left: The *Queen Elizabeth*, painted in gray, makes her secret dash from the Clyde to New York, photographed by a sailor from a destroyer in mid-Atlantic. (J&C McCutcheon Collection)

Above right: Moran tugs dock the *Queen Elizabeth* in this photo from March 1940. She has made a secret dash from Scotland and now awaits further orders. Already idle, the *Normandie* is on the right. (Frank O. Braynard Collection)

Above left: Three giants: the *Normandie* (top), *Queen Mary* (middle) and *Queen Elizabeth* (bottom) await their calls to duty in this classic scene from March 1940. Italy's still-neutral *Vulcania* is at the bottom, berthed at Pier 92. (Frank O. Braynard Collection)

Right: Another view of the three largest liners yet built, also dating from March 1940. (James Sesta Collection)

Above: Following the *Queen Mary* by six months, the *Queen Elizabeth* slips out of New York harbor in November 1940, bound for a long voyage to Australia and the important task of carrying troops. (Frank O. Braynard Collection)

Left: Beginning in 1942, the *Queens* were transferred back to the North Atlantic, carrying 15,000 soldiers per trip. (Frank O. Braynard Collection)

In July 1943, the *Queen Mary* established an all-time record: 16,683 passengers and crew aboard a single ship. (Everett Viez Collection)

Right: During the war, the *Queens* sailed on zigzag courses, blacked out and with radio silence. Hitler offered a special reward to the U-boat captain that could sink the giant ships with 15,000 troops and 1,000 crew aboard. (Cunard Line)

Above left: All arrivals and departures during the war were high security and the movements of the *Queens* were top-secret. (Cunard Line)

Below left: A twin-bedded first class cabin could sleep up to eighteen during the war; a suite was rearranged for twenty-two officers. (Cunard Line)

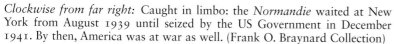

Clockwise from far right: Caught in limbo: the *Normandie* waited at New York from August 1939 until seized by the US Government in December 1941. By then, America was at war as well. (Frank O. Braynard Collection)

During the War, there were eight sessions of breakfast of twenty minutes each; no lunch; and eight sessions of dinner, also twenty minutes each. (Cunard Line)

While being hurriedly stripped and converted for 15,000-capacity troopship duties, the *Normandie* caught fire on the cold afternoon of February 9, 1942. She was berthed at the French Line terminal at Pier 88, at the foot of West 48th Street. (Everett Viez Collection)

For two and a half years, the ship's luxurious innards were empty, silent and indeed very lonely. (Frank O. Braynard Collection)

Above left: The *Normandie* burned well into the night and soon began to list. (Cronican-Arroyo Collection)

Below left: In the early morning hours of February 10, the great ship – heavily overloaded with firefighters' water – rolled over and capsized. She was soon declared a complete loss to the war effort. (Cronican-Arroyo Collection)

Right: French Line gangways were yanked from the pier as the ship began to capsize. (Frank O. Braynard Collection)

On her side, the *Normandie* looked grotesque – 'like a big, dead whale', said one onlooker. (Author's Collection)

Above left: Systematically and carefully, the 83,000-ton ship had to be cut down and slowly refloated. (Frank O. Braynard Collection)

Above right: Grotesquely, her starboard propellers poke above the Hudson River waters. (Frank O. Braynard Collection)

Left: Towed down the Hudson, the hulk of the *Normandie* was laid up (in Brooklyn) until the fall of 1946. She was then declared surplus. This photo shows her top deck looking forward. (Cronican-Arroyo Collection)

Above: Last rites: the last pieces of the *Normandie* are being scrapped at Port Newark, New Jersey, in this view dating from the summer of 1947. (Frank O. Braynard Collection)

Right: Slowly, with her upperworks and upper decks removed, the 1,029-foot-long ship was pumped out and righted. Part of Pier 88 had to be removed in the process. (Frank O. Braynard Collection)

RENEWAL & REBIRTH
THE POST-WAR YEARS

New York harbor, the great terminus for the Atlantic liners on the western side of the ocean, was booming not only in the years of the Second World War, but afterward as well. In the late 1940s, the world, and even America itself, was rebuilding, refitting, even rethinking. It was a new, finally peaceful and optimistic age. The dark days of fighting and battles and losses and war bonds and blackouts were over (annoyingly, however, quite severe rationing would continue in Britain). The commercial, fare-paying Atlantic liner trade resumed almost immediately, in the summer of 1945. Norway's 13,000-ton *Stavangerfjord* resumed sailings that August, the first commercial liner since the war's end.

Noted author Harold Evans first went to New York a decade or so later, in 1956, aboard Cunard's *Franconia*. 'The whole family,' he later wrote, 'waved me off with a simulation of cheerfulness as the ship steamed out of Liverpool harbor. We were nine days at sea, most of which, one gale excepting, I spent crouched on deck over a chess board. We were all rushed to the foredeck, he recalled five decades later, for the tricky navigation of entry into New York harbor.' He wrote, 'This, though, is the only way to arrive in America, as the first Virginians and Pilgrims did. The millions who now come by air every year to JFK and Newark miss the euphoria of landfall as the sea mists dissolve into Lady Liberty and syncopating skyscrapers, and soon enough you are tasting the cosmopolitan street life of the city.' And he added, P. G. Wodehouse said, 'That arriving in New York was like going to heaven without the bother and expense of dying.'

Cunard, still the leader of the pack, was ready and back in business in 1946. The giant *Queen Elizabeth* – fresh in commercial colors and outfitted to every last chair and table and upper bunk down in tourist class on D Deck – finally had her commercial maiden crossing that October. It was five days from Southampton and Cherbourg, and then the tug and fireboat reception all the way up the Lower Bay and along the Hudson River to the north side of Pier 90. The great ship, capped by her twin orange-red and black funnels, towered above the gritty warehouses and factories of West 50th Street. From their glorious, temple-like headquarters, at the very bottom of Broadway, Cunard agents were accepting reservations. The 2,233-bed *Elizabeth* was booking to absolute capacity on almost every trip. The *Queen Mary*, also refitted and back to her original, almost Odeon-style glamour, was back in the summer of 1947. Finally, after waiting for seven years, for all of the hideous war, they had their two-ship, Atlantic express service. Businessmen and movie stars loved it – they could be in London or Paris in five days and have a rest, cocktails, long dinners and maybe a massage in between. European royalty as well as Hollywood royalty were soon among the regulars. This select group also included members of the Soviet delegations, traveling to the United Nations for meetings and conferences, but – as fine, abiding, no-frills party members – traveling down in tourist class.

One by one, the surviving earlier liners were revived – the sparklingly fresh *America* in November 1946, Holland's splendid *Nieuw Amsterdam* a year later and, returned to them from generous American keepers, Italy's *Saturnia* and *Vulcania* (and together with the *Conte Biancamano* and *Conte Grande*) were restored. Then there was the superb, gourmet *Ile de France* – modernized and face-lifted with two instead of her original three funnels – back on Le Havre–New York duties in July 1949. The glamour was returning too – film queen Greta Garbo was among her inaugural season passengers.

Steam whistles and electric horns hooted and honked. New York harbor was putting out its red carpet – a brand new ship was arriving. And being just after the dreary, dark days of the Second World War, it was cause to be happy and hopeful. It was August 1947 and, while not a superliner or record-breaking ship, Cunard's 13,300-ton *Media* was arriving in port. Tugs escorted the flag-bedecked ship to her berth along the city's West Side piers. Capped by her sparkling orange-red and black funnel, she was in fact quite significant: she was the first brand-new passenger ship to be built following the war. She symbolized revival. And more new liners, it was confidently reported, would follow in her wake. Her twin sister, the *Parthia*, as an example, was due in New York for the first time in April 1948.

And, of course, new ships were in the works: although small, Sweden's 11,700-ton *Stockholm* had her debut in 1948 while Norway added a new flagship, the *Oslofjord*, a year later. The biggest and possibly most luxurious new post-war liner was Cunard's 34,200-ton *Caronia*. Amongst her indulgent features, every passenger cabin on board had private bathroom facilities. In 1951, Holland added the *Ryndam* and *Maasdam*, which offered vastly improved accommodations but in tourist class. John Tabbut-McCarthy and his family often crossed on the 15,000-ton *Ryndam*. 'We loved the little *Ryndam*. She was intimate – and slower and so offered a longer voyage. It was ten days from, say, Rotterdam to New York with stops at Le Havre, Southampton, sometimes Cobh and at Halifax two days before New York. She carried a very small first class [thirty-nine berths in all] and we always occupied the same upper-deck cabins. Mine was done in green. We'd also have the same table in the small, almost private dining room. The table had, as I remember, wooden lips around the edges and was sprinkled with water in rough seas. There was also a little card room, a smoking room and a bar. There was a little staircase up to first class. The ship had a little pool out on deck and

we'd go to the tourist class lounge to see movies. I also remember the forward lounge, also in tourist class, which had bamboo chairs and floral-print cushions. Princess Margriet, a daughter of Queen Juliana, once sailed on the *Ryndam*. But I remember that other, lesser members of the Dutch royal family preferred the *Noordam* and *Westerdam,* which carried about 150 passengers each and all of them in first class.'

The great glamour and style of Atlantic ocean liner travel was back in full force by the 1950s. A man from Tucson noted, 'In 1953, we went to Europe on the *Ile de France*. What a wonderful ship! But I will never, ever forget the food. The canapés were so lavish and so big that we thought they were dinner!' In upper-deck first class, there were the likes of the Duke and Duchess of Windsor, who sailed the Atlantic on two round trips a year and with ninety-eight pieces of luggage, personal servants, their dogs, and even their own crested china and bed linens. But even in lower-fare tourist class, there was great style. Jane Hawthorne, going to Paris as a student aboard the *Ile de France*, recalled, 'The dinner menu was so extravagant and included Bisque of Lobster, Supreme of Turbot and Truffled Goose Liver. Even the breakfasts were a treat. There was, as I well remember, Skate in Butter Sauce.'

'The great *Nieuw Amsterdam* was one of my favorite Atlantic liners,' said John Tabbutt-McCarthy, 'and I was very fortunate to sail to Europe in her and in first class. I had a huge cabin with two portholes and three easy chairs. I remember that the first class restaurant had a gold leather ceiling. There was great style and a Russian baroness was aboard. But being younger, I always went down to the tourist class bar after dinner and had great fun with all the students.'

Now long retired from a life at sea and living near Sydney, Australia, Liverpool-born and bred Robert Welding was a cook aboard some of Britain's greatest and grandest ocean liners of the late 1950s and '60s. He served on the likes of the *Reina Del Mar*,

Britannic, Caronia, Sylvania and the legendary *Queen Mary* and *Queen Elizabeth*. He sailed to the Caribbean and South America, crossed the North Atlantic to New York as well as Montreal and made three full world cruises. Dedication and lots of hard work, it was also romance, adventure and a young man's dreams come true. He was fifteen when he first put to sea on the west coast of South America-routed *Reina Del Mar* in 1958. 'It was a wonderful life for a relatively poor, working-class young man in 1950s Britain,' he said. 'It was a great opportunity. It was also totally exciting. Yes, it was lots of hard work, but I traveled everywhere. Family and friends back in Liverpool used to gather round and listen to my tales of faraway places. Many men and some women went to sea to escape their home situation – and anything was more glamorous than England at that time,' remembered Welding. 'The wages at sea were then one-third greater than those ashore and you actually could save money and possibly buy a house, a small one, of course. But you had to avoid the gambling amongst the crew. That could be deadly – all your wages gone even! Of course, going to sea was a wonderful opportunity to travel and see the world and meet different people and to buy things. Once, I came home with two Hawaiian shirts, all flowery and which were so unique in the UK back then. So, it was a chance to shop as well, to buy things such as portable radios, records in Manhattan and high-quality clothes. Many things were then affordable on a seaman's wages. I bought my first Fruit-of-the-Loom jockey shorts in New York for $1.50 for four in a packet. They were so much better than the old-fashioned, heavy cotton underpants we had in England. Fruit-of-the-Loom was very comfortable polished cotton. I was earning $30 a month in 1959, which was a decent wage in the UK then,' he added. 'I could buy a lamb's wool sports jacket, trousers and shoes for $10. I felt very smart – and very proud. I had my Duffel coat [long top coat with a hood on top] bought from the Army & Navy Shop for my rovings around New York City. I also bought khaki trousers, which cost $2 a pair in Manhattan, but which were eye-openers back in England. I also bought jeans and soft moccasins. And I also bought Pyrex pots and plates in New York. It was then $3 for three pots. Like me, many of the crew loved Woolworth's.'

As an apprentice cook, Robert Welding rotated among many of the great Cunard liners of the day. He added, 'We worked almost the whole of the year on the *Caronia*. We had five weeks off out of fifty-two. You could take leave, of course, but it was best to stay with the ship, stick to the Company schedule. On board the *Queen Mary* and *Queen Elizabeth*, it was three round trips to New York and back on and then one round trip off. As a cook, I lived in cabins that had two bunks, two stools, a washbasin, two wardrobes and a bare steel floor that was painted. They were actually very tight and quite dreary. A board was often placed over the washbasin and that created a table. There was forced-air ventilation, but – in lower-deck quarters – it was often difficult to sleep comfortably. The older liners absorbed more heat in port, as I remember, and so retained more heat and had less ventilation. On warm, summer nights, we slept on deck, on the forward hatch, on the old *Britannic*. A canvas tarp was put up and we brought up mattresses. On the *Caronia*, on her cruises in tropical waters, we slept in rattan lounge chairs under the countless stars of those warm nights. There was great shipboard discipline and rules at Cunard, of course. Every morning at 10, the crew quarters were inspected and checked for even the slightest dust. Of course, it was usually sweltering and dust was inevitable. It was all about discipline and order. We knew, however, to avoid eye contact with the top officers and so not to be noticed. There was a Master-at-Arms that was usually either ex-Royal Navy or ex-police. There was a sort of little police station on board and this included a lock-up somewhere, a kind of a brig.'

Above and right: Free of Nazi U-boat attack, the gray-painted *Queen Mary* returns to Southampton in May 1945, her first call there in nearly six years, since August 1939. (J&C McCutcheon Collection)

Left: Triumph: the *Queen Elizabeth* brings home one of the first official waves of returning US troops in this scene from summer 1945. (J&C McCutcheon Collection)

Top: The veteran, thirty-one-year-old *Aquitania* continues her duties: returning American servicemen to Pier 86, New York, in this photo from the fall of 1945. (J&C McCutcheon Collection)

Above: Millions returned by ship to the docks in New York in the years following the end of the Second World War. There were the troops, the wounded, refugees, displaced persons and the last inmates from the Nazi death camps. (J&C McCutcheon Collection)

Right: The *Queen Elizabeth* enters dry dock at Southampton in October 1946. (J&C McCutcheon Collection)

Below left: In 1946, the noble *Queen Elizabeth* was the first superliner to be decommissioned and was restored for peacetime luxury service. She is shown here having her stern painted black on the Clyde off Gourock in June 1946. (J&C McCutcheon Collection)

Below right: Cunard had to lease a small airport near Southampton to sort the furniture in the post-war restoration of the *Queen Elizabeth*. This view shows her newly fitted-out shop on the Promenade Deck. (J&C McCutcheon Collection)

Above left: From the late 1940s through the late 1950s, Atlantic liners again enjoyed great prosperity and popularity. It all seemed as if it would go on forever. The *Queen Elizabeth* berths at Southampton at the end of another full crossing. (J&C McCutcheon Collection)

Above right: The beautiful Italian liner *Andrea Doria* was rammed in fog in July 1956 by the Swedish liner *Stockholm* and is shown here, sinking, photographed from the *Ile de France*. (J&C McCutcheon Collection)

Left: A rare meeting of the *Queens*. (J&C McCutcheon Collection)

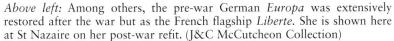

Above left: Among others, the pre-war German *Europa* was extensively restored after the war but as the French flagship *Liberte*. She is shown here at St Nazaire on her post-war refit. (J&C McCutcheon Collection)

Above right: The *Liberte* eastbound at Plymouth in the early 1950s.

Right: The liners came and went at New York with timed regularity, even during strikes. Here we see the giant *Queen Elizabeth* arriving at Pier 90 without tugs. She rammed the pier as she berthed but the damage was slight. The Italian liner *Cristoforo Colombo* (shown bottom) was also slightly damaged as she berthed, in this view from May 1964. (J&C McCutcheon Collection)

Left: America produced the most brilliant superliner of the immediate post-war years: the speedy, highly advanced, innovative *United States.* (United States Lines)

Above: The maiden arrival into New York harbor of the brilliant *United States* in a photo dated June 1952. (United States Lines)

Right: The *Queens* were the most popular and profitable pair of superliners in the 1950s. They earned millions for Cunard and for Britain itself. They would arrive in New York on Tuesdays and then sail on Wednesdays and then reverse ships the following week. Here we see the *Queen Mary* passing under the Verrazano Narrows Bridge, then under construction. (J&C McCutcheon Collection)

Below left: The *Queens* were almost always fully booked on their crossings, even in deep winter, in the 1950s. First class fares for the five-day crossings began at $400 in 1960; from $250 for cabin class and $175 in lower-deck tourist class. An 'Atlantic Interlude' was a chance for five days of rest and relaxation aboard. (J&C McCutcheon Collection)

Below right: High summer along Luxury Liner Row. In a view from September 4, 1957, there are the *Britannic*, *Queen Mary* and *Mauretania* of Cunard; the *Flandre* of French Line; the *Olympia*, Greek Line; the *United States*; and *Independence* of American Export Lines. (Port Authority of New York & New Jersey)

Far left: Wintery afternoon: the brand-new *France* is in mid-Hudson, departing on her eastbound maiden voyage while (from left to right) the *Cristoforo Colombo* of Italian Line as well as the *America* and *United States* are at dock. (Cronican-Arroyo Collection)

Left: A painting by James Flood, showing a marvelous selection of funnels in Luxury Liner Row. Ships include the *Independence*, the *United States*, and the *Queen Mary*. (James Flood)

Below: Sea Coach Transatlantic Lines, Inc, designed two superliners for the transatlantic trade. Each could carry 6,000 passengers and were of 90,000 tons. The ships were never built. (Author's Collection)

$50. FARE TO EUROPE

Above left: The brand-new HMS *Sheffield* salutes the *Queen Mary*, with the Shah of Persia aboard, in 1955. (J&C McCutcheon Collection)

Below left: As many as 5,000 visitors and well-wishers would see off 2,000 passengers aboard the likes of the Cunard *Queens* on either side of the Atlantic. (J&C McCutcheon Collection)

Right: Majestic and evocative, the grand *Queen Mary* sails outbound, passing the magical New York City skyline, as the *Queen Elizabeth* sets sail from Southampton's Ocean Terminal. (J&C McCutcheon Collection)

Left: Shipboard splendor: the magnificent first class main lounge aboard the *Queen Elizabeth*. It had the enticing smell of leather, fresh flowers and furniture polish. (J&C McCutcheon Collection)

Above: The main restaurant aboard Holland America's *Nieuw Amsterdam*. The ceiling was done in Moroccan leather, the chandeliers were made by Murano and there was live music each evening. (Holland America Line)

Above left: Hollywood glamour on the high seas: a suite aboard the 1938-built *Nieuw Amsterdam*. It was pure Ginger Rogers! (Holland America Line)

Above right: Fair weather: out on deck on a summer crossing aboard the *United States*. (United States Lines)

Right: The *Queen Elizabeth* being refuelled in Southampton in readiness for another transatlantic voyage. (J&C McCutcheon Collection)

Above left: Passengers often rested on the way to Europe – a good book, a blanket and the tea trolley at 4. (United States Lines)

Left: The Duke and Duchess of Windsor arrive at Cherbourg for the December 16, 1952 westbound sailing of the *Queen Mary*. (J&C McCutcheon Collection)

Right: Celebrity guests and passengers: Queen Elizabeth, the Queen Mother, crosses on board the *Queen Elizabeth* in October 1954. (J&C McCutcheon Collection)

Above left: Actor John Wayne on the starboard bridge of the *United States* with Commodore John Anderson. (United States Lines)

Above right: Dean Martin, Tony Curtis, Janet Leigh and Jerry Lewis on board the *Queen Elizabeth* in the late 1950s. (J&C McCutcheon Collection)

Right: Actor Dennis O'Keefe arrives from New York on the *Queen Elizabeth* on June 18, 1957. (J&C McCutcheon Collection)

THE LAST SPEED QUEEN: *UNITED STATES*

On a winter's night in 2010, a dozen or so of us sat down to a fine dinner in a midtown Manhattan restaurant. The purpose was friendly and chatty, but intended, as part of the SS *United States* Trust, to save that great, but long decaying and neglected liner from, well, the scrappers. The Trust's mission, assuming they could come up with hundreds of millions of dollars needed for renovations and the likes of visitor safety components, was to see the 990-foot-long liner moored along New York City's West Side waterfront as a grand museum – and most likely, a hotel and convention center and collection of shops as well. It was all very spirited, very positive, almost convincing. We finished the meal and headed home with the faint feeling that the ship herself might be appearing along the Hudson River and very soon. It was a time, quite coincidentally, when rumors were again plentiful and flying that the ship's owners, Norwegian Cruise Line, and their Malaysian parent, the Genting Corporation, were actively planning to unload the idle ship. They had her since 2002, but nothing had come to pass of earlier plans to revive her as, say, a cruise ship plying the Hawaiian islands route. Now instead, there was talk of Indian scrap merchants visiting the liner at her Philadelphia moorings. There were suggestions that she could bring as much as $4 million in scrap value. She was, after all, costing something in the neighborhood of $500,000-plus a year in upkeep – for the likes of dockage fees and the occasional pumping out of rain water.

William Francis Gibbs, America's finest naval architect, had long dreamed of the United States having a great superliner of its own. He had made numerous proposals, drawings and sketches beginning in the 1920s for record-breaking ships flying the red, white and blue. But it was not until the Second World War, and especially as the Cunard *Queens* were ferrying 15,000 troops per crossing at the height of the hostilities, that the US Government realized the great importance of a big, fast liner as a military transport. The role as a flag-carrying commercial liner was almost secondary. Gibbs was commissioned to design what would be the most technologically advanced Atlantic liner of all time. Known as the 'the Big Ship' project, his designs began in earnest in 1946. The ship would cost over $70 million, a staggering amount for the time, and would be built at Newport News, Virginia.

Commissioned in the spring of 1952, the *United States* was shielded in US Government secrecy with regard to many components, but still fascinated the public. There were 125,000 pieces of chinaware on board, 4,000 blankets and her overall design required 1.2 million blueprints. In every way, she was an amazing success, a tour de force of post-Second World War triumph and distinction. During her trials, for example, it was later revealed that she made 20 knots, but in reverse, and that she reached a speed of some 43 knots. She was assuredly the fastest, most powerful liner ever and had an average speed of some 36 knots during her westbound maiden voyage. For the next decade, her success was assured. Everyone, it seemed, wanted to sail aboard the 'world's fastest liner'.

Within, she was a ship of high, 1950s modernity. Even the artwork in the first class restaurant was made of aluminum. Perhaps one of the best-known stories about the 53,329-ton, 1,928-passenger *United States* involved her extremely high safety standards. There was, it was often said, absolutely no wood on board except in the butcher's block and the piano.

'The *United States* was a ship, as I remember her, of great, shining linoleum. She was just gleaming everywhere,' remembered John Tabbutt-McCarthy, who was a regular traveler on Atlantic liners in the 1950s and '60s. 'You could eat off the floors on the

United States. She had big public rooms and where all the chairs were bolted to the floor as I recall. In the cabins, there were beds with protective ridges along the sides, lots of gray and other muted colors, and metallic furniture. But I do remember that many thought that the *United States* was a ship that lacked great feeling. She was just racing back and forth across the Atlantic. Many preferred the smaller, slower *America*, which offered a longer, more leisurely voyage to and from Europe.'

The 1950s brought out something of a last parade of sorts of new Atlantic liners: ships such as the *Independence* and *Constitution*, the *Flandre*, the *Olympia*, the *Andrea Doria* and *Cristoforo Colombo*, the *Kungsholm* and the *Bergensfjord*. The biggest and most extravagant of the newbuilds of the late 1950s was the *France*, the last of the French 'floating palaces'. Just as she was under construction and despite the dramatic, very intrusive appearance of the jet, ideas for new passenger ships, including superliners, were still plentiful and optimistic. Along with the likes of the *Rotterdam*, *Leonardo da Vinci*, *Empress of Canada* and the aforementioned 66,300-ton *France*, there was actually far more ambitious plans. In July 1959, New York City-based businessman and hotel owner Hyman B. Cantor signed a contract with a shipyard in Hamburg to study the possible construction of twin 90,000-ton liners for the North Atlantic. These ships, it would seem, would break every record in size and distinction. They would have accommodations for 6,000 passengers and crews of 1,350, and service speeds of 34 knots. It was envisioned that they would sail the North Atlantic, between New York, Zeebrugge and an undetermined port in Germany (but most likely to be Cuxhaven for Hamburg). Catering would be on a cafeteria style and the lowest fare, not including meals, was put at $75. The two ships would cost, it was estimated, $160 million to build. The first of them, to be named *Peace,* would be delivered in August 1962, with the second ship, the *Goodwill,* following in August 1963. Expectedly, the main problem was the financing.

Meanwhile, two months later, in September 1959, businessman Edgar Detwiler had approached a Dutch shipyard for the construction of no less than four even larger passenger liners. Construction of the first was to start with a year, during 1960, and completion expected in 1963. Mr Detwiler's ships would be 120,000 gross tons and measure 1,275 feet in length and 130 feet in width. They would have a service speed of 35 knots and carry 8,000 passengers, with 2,000 crew. They would be slightly less expensive than Mr Cantor's ships with fares starting at $65 and including meals. They would sail for the newly created American-European Lines, fly the Dutch flag and would be named *United Nations*, *New Yorker*, *Lisbon* and *Hollander*. The first pair would sail the North Atlantic, between New York, Cobh, Plymouth and Amsterdam; the second set would run on the mid-Atlantic, between New York, Lisbon and, on some sailings, to either Naples or Genoa. The ships would use the new, innovative, engines-aft design.

Interesting, even fascinating, neither of these ambitious schemes came to pass. A model of Cantor's projected ship sat for many years in the lobby of the now long-bygone Dixie Hotel in midtown Manhattan, but was last reported to have found a home just across the Hudson, on the campus of Stevens Institute of Technology in Hoboken.

The Atlantic liners of the 1950s and '60s were the last of a great breed and remain iconic, often deeply revered in retrospect. In late 2009, the beloved Holland America liner *Rotterdam*, that last nationally built flagship and Atlantic liner built for the illustrious Holland America Line, opened – and right in Rotterdam harbor, no less – as a grand memorial to the past. After seemingly endless and immensely high spending, she was now refitted and restyled as a floating hotel, convention center and, rather expectedly, museum. She was a grand keepsake of a grand era – and happily one of the most cherished liners of that final fleet of Atlantic ships created in the 1950s and '60s. 'We are lucky, very lucky, to have her back. She has been saved,' said marine artist Stephen Card.

TWILIGHT FOR THE ATLANTIC LINERS

In the fading light of a January afternoon, we sailed off from Miami, still sprouting its wings in its growth as the world's busiest cruise port, on board the *Norway*. Flags fluttered, the whistles sounded and we were off – well over 2,000 of us on a weeklong escape to the sun-drenched eastern Caribbean, to St Thomas and St Maarten and then to Great Stirrup Cay, a so-called 'private island' in the nearby Bahamas. It was all quite exciting. The year was 1981. The *Norway*, then listed as the largest ocean liner and certainly the biggest cruise liner ever, had been rather gloriously reworked from her previous, quite famous life as the *France*, the last of the grand French transatlantic liners. Few ships have ever had a more successful, mid-life change. For a time, we were encouraged, thinking that another out-of-work super ship, the *United States*, might be soon plying tropic waters as well. Why couldn't she too be converted?

Atlantic superliners were having their last gasps of profitable air in the 1950s. But change and subsequent decline and demise were just around the corner. By the 1960s, it was just about all over. After considerable debate and discussion, the *France* seemed the logical successor to the older, aging French liners, the *Ile de France* and the *Liberte*, which were soon destined for distant scrapyards. A big liner, it was felt by her French underwriters and supporters in Paris, could replace both ships, lead the French Line into the distant future and, of course, keep the Tricolor proudly flying amidst the likes of British, German, Dutch, Italian and even American competitors. The French Government – who would pay a big chunk of the building costs – was excited. From its headquarters along the Rue Auber, the French Line prepared endless preliminary press and promotional material. Yes, at 1,035 feet from stem to stern, the new ship would be the longest liner yet – and, rather triumphantly, would exceed Cunard's beloved *Queen Elizabeth* by four feet. She'd be luxurious, well served and continue the French tradition of having the very best kitchens on the Atlantic. And she would be fast, but not a record-breaker – there was simply no need for that. Besides, the Blue Ribbon-champ *United States* had lots of reserve power just in case. The *France* was, of course, acclaimed as the best-fed liner on the Atlantic in the 1960s. 'A travel agent highly recommended the *France* to my grandmother. He told her that she would not get seasick because the *France* was the longest liner in the world,' recalled John Tabbutt-McCarthy. 'My grandmother booked the *France*, but was sick for the entire five-day crossing from Le Havre to New York. She never saw the dining room. Myself, I recall that the *France* had the most fabulous food, even in tourist class.'

The *France* endured for twelve years, until laid up in 1974, a victim mostly of soaring operational costs and the French Government's reluctance to further subsidize the ship. The Italian Government built a pair of big liners, the 45,000-ton sisters *Michelangelo* and *Raffaello* in as late as 1965. Prodded by unionized workers both ashore and afloat, they were misfits in a waning mid-Atlantic trade. Sadly, they never earned a single lira in profit in their ten years of service. John Tabbutt-McCarthy crossed westbound from the Mediterranean to New York in the summer of 1968 on board the *Raffaello*. 'She was an ultra-modern ship then. There was linoleum on the bridge,' he recalled. 'She had great food and service in first class, and had those two great, cage-like funnels. But she and the *Michelangelo* had a different style. They weren't quite as smart, I felt, as the earlier Italian liners of the 1950s.'

May 9, 1967 proved to be one of the most dramatic days in Cunard peacetime history. The great curtain was finally coming down: a simple, but clear-cut message was flashed to the commanders of both *Queens* that the ships would soon be no more. The *Mary* would go that September; the *Elizabeth* in October 1968. Within a decade, Cunard had plunged from having twelve Atlantic liners to three. John Tabbutt-McCarthy was aboard the great *Queen Mary* in the summer of 1967, aboard one of her final crossings. 'She still had a certain grandeur. She had the grandest first class dining room I'd ever seen. There was a wonderful breakfast menu and everything was done in Aspic such as great hams with little olives. The chefs were huge men, very corpulent and always seemed to have huge arms with big tattoos. There was also a glorious indoor pool for first class,' he remembered. 'But the ship had actually gotten quite tatty. There was lots of what I call Queen Mother furniture – aged chairs and tables that looked as if they'd been scratched by dogs. There were also lots of sandpapered materials from the 1930s and 1940s. I had a cabin down on B Deck that included salt and fresh water taps. The ship was quite empty and, on our crossing, rolled and rolled and rolled. Captain Treasure-Jones was in command and I remember visiting the bridge as well as the engine room.'

Still stately and regal, the *Queen Mary* – by then the last of the Atlantic's three-stackers – left New York for the last time on September 22, 1967. There was enormous interest in her farewells, for no ship better symbolized the glamour of the transatlantic era – and now its demise. She had been the most successful of all superliners, the most majestic Cunarder then in service, a ship heroic in war and perhaps the grandest and best-loved ship in all of Cunard's rich history. Tugs, ferries and yachts escorted her downriver. Helicopters buzzed overhead and newspapers, television and radio widely reported on this 'last farewell'. She was leaving behind a splendid record: 1,000 crossings, 3.7 million miles, 2 million passengers and revenues of some $600 million in her thirty-one years. But now she was out of place, an anachronism in the new jet age.

Amidst several offers and proposals, including Japanese scrap merchants with $3.25 million, an unlikely candidate won out in the end. The city of Long Beach, California, wanted her as a tourist attraction and bought her with a bid of $3.45 million. The great Atlantic liner would go into retirement on the Pacific. After a $72 million makeover and upgrading (mostly for more stringent safety standards), which was three times more than she had cost to build thirty-odd years before, she opened as a moored tourist attraction in May 1971. There were mixed reviews, however. Some buffs and historians were delighted that she had been preserved, others were horrified by such touches as hot dog stands along the Promenade Deck. Her success, over some forty years to date, has been varied and there have been some tense times, even when Asian scrappers have taken a look at her.

The twenty-eight-year-old *Queen Elizabeth* was retired in October 1968, but did not fare as well. It was intended to make her into the East Coast version of the *Queen Mary*, but berthed at Fort Lauderdale. Optimistically, this time Cunard held an 85 per cent share in the project. But nothing came to pass except mismanagement, scandals and court battles. The faded *Elizabeth* sat idle, rusting further in the often fierce Florida sun. Japanese scrap merchants were again in the picture. Late in the summer of 1970, however, Taiwanese shipping tycoon C. Y. Tung bought her for restoration and conversion into a combination cruise ship-floating university. Renamed *Seawise University*, she was sent to Hong Kong for extensive renovations. But on January 9, 1972, nearing the very end of her renewal, she caught fire (five separate fires on the same day, in fact) and soon turned into a blistering inferno. Overloaded with firefighters' water, she capsized the next day. Arson has never been ruled out. The Japanese scrappers again reappeared, and this time they won the contract and cut up the remains. By 1974, the former *Queen Elizabeth* was gone from Hong Kong harbor, a tragic ending for an outstanding ship.

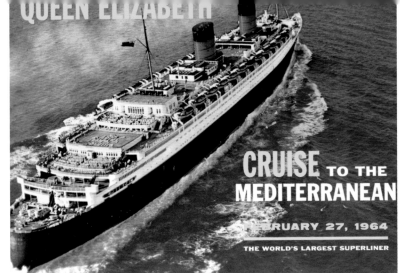

CRUISE TO THE MEDITERRANEAN

FEBRUARY 27, 1964

THE WORLD'S LARGEST SUPERLINER

Above left: The airlines began to make serious inroads amongst transatlantic travelers by the mid-1950s, but the most decisive intrusion were the first jet flights in October 1958. (J&C McCutcheon Collection)

Above right: By the mid-1960s, the big liners were big dinosaurs. They were deserted in winter, half-full in normally peak summers. Sent cruising, the *Queen Elizabeth* and *Queen Mary* were dismal failures due to a lack of air-conditioning and facilities for more than seven days at sea. (J&C McCutcheon Collection)

Left and far left: The *France*, the *Michelangelo* and *Raffaello* and then the *Queen Elizabeth 2* were the last big Atlantic liners of their time. (Author's Collection)

Left: The *Michelangelo* berthed at New York, dressed overall. (J&C McCutcheon Collection)

Below left: By the mid-1970s, almost all the Atlantic liners had drifted off to retirement – the scrapyards mostly, but some, often ill-advised attempts at cruising. Here we see the *United States*, which was retired in November 1969, making one of her final departures from New York. (Norman Knebel Collection)

Right: The *United States* has been laid up for over forty years, the longest phase for any passenger liner. She is seen here at Norfolk, VA, in a view dating from June 1979. (Author's Collection)

Above: An empty, silent ship: the foredecks of the *United States* as seen from the bow in a photo from 1992. (Author's Collection)

Left: Gentle retirement: the cherished *Queen Mary* lives on in secure afterlife as a museum and hotel at Long Beach, California. (Hotel Queen Mary)

Above, left and right: The *Queen Elizabeth*, as the renamed *Seawise University*, did not fare as well. She burned out and then capsized in Hong Kong harbor in January 1972. Later, she was scrapped on the spot, her remains becoming razor blades and Toyotas. (J&C McCutcheon Collection)

ONE LAST CLASSIC ATLANTIC LINER
QUEEN ELIZABETH 2

On a warm day in March 2010, I saw the *Queen Elizabeth 2* in an unlikely setting: laid up and idle at Port Rashid in distant Dubai. Our cruise ship, the *Crystal Serenity*, berthed just next to her, the view of her stern. The forty-one-year-old *Queen* had again been in the news. After a wild flourish of extravagant spending, building and highly enthusiastic planning for the future, Dubai was caught in the net of the great international recession. The otherwise tiny emirate, capped by the likes of the world's tallest building, the then-just-opened, 162-storey Burj Khalifa, was in debt, deep debt, estimated at over $60 billion. Bankers and creditors had ordered a massive downsizing, a grand reduction, the shedding of holdings and properties. Among these was the 963-foot-long *Queen Elizabeth 2*, which, in that final fling of

extravagant and excessive spending, had been purchased from the Carnival Corporation, itself the hugely wealthy parent of the historic Cunard Line, for $100 million. In 2008, the aging ship was then worth, perhaps, $5–7 million on, say, the bustling Indian scrap market (where great numbers of the world's ships were then going to die, to finish their days in the hands of $1-a-day demolition crews along the remote beaches of Alang, an otherwise unknown spot north-west of Mumbai), but which fetched $100 million. 'It was her name that warranted the extra $95 million or so,' said one fan of the great Cunarder. 'Dubai wanted something famous, very famous, and in shipping, there was nothing better than the *QE2*. She was the most famous ocean liner in the world. She was also a great symbol.'

On a winter's morning a year before, in 2009, I visited the midtown Manhattan offices of a design firm. They were designing the interiors for a series of new cruise ships. They wanted to chat, to discuss the great link between landside and shipboard decoration. But more interesting, resting on a conference room table was a 15-inch-tall model of a recreation of the *QE2*'s iconic funnel. This was not a rebuilt version, but a newly constructed one – quite similar in style and painted in Cunard colors, but with panoramic windows and terraces for the luxury penthouses that would be inside. The original funnel in the rebuilding and refitting of the ship was to be lifted ashore and placed, as some kind of sentimental memento, as a parking lot monument. The ship was to be restyled as a luxury residence, hotel, museum and carnival of shops and entertainment venues by the local Nakheel Corporation and moored on another extravagant project, Palm Island. She would be just another of Dubai's stellar structures and attractions. But then there was the recession and it all went off the boards.

Dubai struggled and there was a brief plan to move the *QE2* to Capetown for use as a floating hotel during the World Cup. But that idea later went by the boards as well, leaving the liner without a future. When I saw her, and while re-registered to Port Vila on Vanuatu (a comparatively unknown 'flag of convenience' in the South Pacific), she seemed untouched. While the Cunard name along the side had been painted out, she was giving off some plumes of smoke from her orange-red and black funnel and was well lighted by night. The likes of her funnel, promenade windows and bridge front were aglow. She was now in the hands of a maintenance crew of sixty, all Egyptians hired by Nakheel to look after the otherwise silent ship. In high, Dubai summer, she sits under brutal forces: temperatures as high as 130 degrees and humidity of as much as 85 per cent. These can be hideously intrusive to a laid-up liner.

There were more than a few sad faces and even tears when the *QE2* went off to Dubai in November 2008. Quite simply, many were sad to see the great ship go, even if she had been around for thirty-eight years and sailed more miles, carried more passengers and visited more ports than any other Atlantic superliner. She was, according to all the record books, the most successful, long-lasting, far-traveling liner of all time. Cunard should have been pleased and very proud. Even the Queen herself came down to the Southampton Docks, in June 2008, to say good-bye. Prince Philip was there for the final departure, a two-week, heavily booked cruise from Southampton out through the Mediterranean and Suez to Dubai. The classic song *Sentimental Journey* seemed apt. And yes, there were more tears on the very last night.

When Cunard was faced with replacing the aging *Queen Mary* in the late 1950s, they were confused, if slightly, at first. Things had changed after all: the intrusive jet had begun flying the Atlantic and, within six months, by mid-1959, had stolen two-thirds of the all trans-ocean clientele. If not doomed entirely, big liners were facing a different future, playing a different role, dealing with varied economics. At first, the classically traditional and conservative company, from its stately headquarters along the Mersey in Liverpool, planned a three-class liner, the *Q3* project. But that idea was soon scrapped and replaced by a ship that would represent the 'new', trendier Cunard.

With nearly 125 years in the Atlantic passenger ship business, Cunard had done some serious rethinking during the early 1960s. Traditional designs for a replacement for both *Queens* were discarded. Indeed, the days of the full-time Atlantic liner were over. Instead, this new giant had to be much more of a floating hotel, a fast, large 'moving resort' that could, having relayed her guests across the Atlantic, with very few changes, sail off to the tropics as a cruise ship. On cruises, passengers enjoyed a seagoing vacation in which the ports were diversions, not destinations. Named *Queen Elizabeth 2* by the Queen in September 1967, this new, 65,800-tonner first appeared on the Southampton–New York run in the spring of 1969. She was immediately deemed a radical departure from her still-well-remembered predecessors. Alone, her single, pipe-like stack proclaimed the differences. The new generation of sales and marketing people at Cunard felt that she should be a complete break with the Cunard of the past. So, instead of the ornately columned lounges and dark wood panels, the triple classes, the mood of an older, almost lost world, there would be a sleek, flashy resort with discos and casinos, top-deck lidos, shopping arcades and befeathered dancing girls in after-dinner revues. Even the traditional Cunard funnel colors of orange-red and black were gone and instead the name Cunard was painted in the same orange-red lettering on the superstructure near the bridge wings. She looked every inch the floating hotel, indeed the modern floating hotel.

Over the years, the *QE2* – as she was dubbed from the very start – has won praises, garnered enormous publicity and has had tremendous popularity. By the time she was decommissioned and handed over to new owners out in Dubai, in November 2008, she had an impeccable record. But in the beginning, in the 1970s especially, there were some grave doubts about her future. Was she too late, a great anachronism? But cleverly, Cunard often balanced her sailings with British Airways – ship one-way and air the other. For the upper grades, there were fancy combinations that included Concorde. It all worked. And then, as the decades passed, the *QE2* became the greatest and grandest symbol of the bygone age of ocean liners. 'She herself was great nostalgia in her final years,' noted a loyalist passenger with forty-five trips aboard the 963-foot-long Cunarder.

Fates of Other Liners …

In her early years, the 2,005-passenger *Queen Elizabeth 2* saw almost all of the remaining Atlantic liners disappear. The brilliant *United States*, after losing her vitally needed US Government subsidy monies, was yanked from service in November 1969. She never sailed again and has remained (at a Philadelphia pier since 1996) in neglected silence for some forty-one years. Holland America Line offered its last Atlantic crossing in September 1971, aboard the beloved *Nieuw Amsterdam* of 1938. North German Lloyd turned completely to cruising that same year while Canadian Pacific ended their liner services altogether. The *France* was abruptly pulled from service in the fall of 1974, a victim of soaring operational costs and, once again, the withdrawal of her much-needed funding from the Ministry of Marine in Paris. Finally, in 1975, the *Michelangelo* and *Raffaello* of the Italian Line were decommissioned after only a decade of service and then the *Leonardo da Vinci* followed a year later, ending Italian Line service altogether.

Cruising largely replaced the crossings of earlier years by the 1960s and '70s. It has become a mega-business such that more people are traveling by ship (2010) than ever before. In the United States, cruising is a $6 billion annual business and eleven million take to the seas each year. Further growth is forecast, highlighted by the construction of the likes of the twin 225,000-ton, 6,400-passenger sisters *Oasis of the Seas* and *Allure of the Seas* for Miami-based Royal Caribbean International.

Above: The Queen named what was said to be the last Atlantic liner, the *Queen Elizabeth 2*, at the ship's launching in September 1967. The *QE2*, as she soon became known, is shown here nearing completion in John Brown's fitting out basin. (J&C McCutcheon Collection)

Below: Despite skeptics' words, the *QE2* went on to become the longest-lasting, most successful big liner of all time. She sailed for thirty-nine years. (J&C McCutcheon Collection)

By the mid-1970s, the *QE2* had undertaken her first world cruise and had been refitted with extra Penthouse cabins directly behind her mast. (J&C McCutcheon Collection)

For one season only, the *QE2* sported a gray hull and superstructure. In 1984, she reverted back to her dark-blue hull, with white superstructure. (J&C McCutcheon Collection)

Above: The *QE2*, which was also the last steam-driven liner on the Atlantic, increasingly became a cherished link to the golden past of the great passenger ships. Her final voyages were fully booked within hours. (J&C McCutcheon)

Right: Over the years, Cunard very sensibly booked the *QE2*'s crossings as one way by sea, the other by air. This included an immensely popular combination with the supersonic Concorde. (British Airways)

MODERN-DAY REVIVAL: *QUEEN MARY 2*

The age of the 'floating palace', that great and grand link to the past, does continue in many ways, however. After the illustrious Cunard Line was sold to the mega-rich, very progressive Carnival Corporation in 1998 (for $600 million), an additional $800 million was allocated to build the largest Atlantic liner ever. She was built at St Nazaire in France and commissioned in late 2003 as the *Queen Mary 2*. At 151,000 tons and carrying up to 2,600 passengers, she has not continued but revived the age of the classic Atlantic crossing. And in the wake of the decommissioning of the stately *Queen Elizabeth 2*, the *Mary 2* has, in many ways, become the most famous ocean liner afloat. She divides her time, of course, with a half-year in crossings to and from New York and the remainder in cruising (including 100 or so day trips around the world).

Sometimes, as she crosses the North Atlantic at over 25 knots, and as I stand at the stern of the 1,132-foot-long *Queen Mary 2*, I pause and reflect. In the churning wake that stretches for miles beyond, I can almost see those earlier floating palaces – the *Kaiser Wilhelm der Grosse*, the first *Mauretania*, *Imperator*, the *Bremen*, the *Normandie* and the earlier *Queen Mary* and *Queen Elizabeth*. They have left an indelible legacy.

Below: Her Majesty Queen Elizabeth II named the biggest Atlantic superliner of all time in ceremonies at Southampton in January 2004. The new ship, named *Queen Mary 2*, weighed in at 151,000 tons and measured 1,132 feet in length. Shown here with *QE2*, Southampton, 2004. (J&C McCutcheon Collection)

Highly popular, the 2,600-passenger *Queen Mary 2* carries the traditions of Atlantic crossings, and of the historic Cunard Line, and is the latest link to that glorious era of the 'floating palaces'. The *QE2* is departing on her final eastbound crossing. The date is October 2008. (Der Scutt Collection)

BIBLIOGRAPHY

Braynard, Frank O. *Lives of the Liners*. New York: Cornell Maritime Press, 1947.

Crowdy, Michael & O'Donoghue, Kevin (editors). *Marine News*. Kendal, Cumbria, England: World Ship Society 1963–2009.

Devol, George & Cassidy, Thomas (editors). *Ocean & Cruise News*. Stamford, Connecticut: World Ocean & Cruise Liner Society, 1980–2009.

Dunn, Laurence. *Passenger Liners*. Southampton, England: Adlard Coles Ltd, 1961.

— *Passenger Liners* (revised edition). Southampton, England: Adlard Coles Ltd, 1965.

Haws, Duncan. *Merchant Fleets: Cunard Line*. Hereford, England: TCL Publications, 1987.

Mayes, William. *Cruise Ships* (revised edition). Windsor, England: Overview Press Ltd, 2009.

Miller, William H. *British Ocean Liners: A Twilight Era 1960–85*. New York: W. W. Norton & Co., 1986.

— *Crossing the Atlantic*. Portland, Oregon: Graphic Arts Books, 2005.

— *The First Great Ocean Liners in Photographs: 1897–1927*. New York, New York: Dover Publications Inc., 1984.

— *German Ocean Liners of the 20th Century*. Wellingborough, Northamptonshire, England, 1989.

— *The Great Luxury Liners 1927–54*. New York: Dover Publications Inc., 1981.

— *Ocean Liner Chronicles*. London: Carmania Press Ltd, 2001.

— *Pictorial Encyclopedia of Ocean Liners, 1864–1994*. Mineola, New York: Dover Publications Inc., 1995.

— *Picture History of American Passenger Ships*. Mineola, New York: Dover Publications Inc., 2001.

— *Picture History of British Ocean Liners*. Mineola, New York: Dover Publications Inc., 2001.

— *Picture History of the Cunard Line 1840–1990*. New York: Dover Publications Inc., 1991.

— *Picture History of German & Dutch Passenger Ships*. New York: Dover Publications Inc., 2002.

— *Picture History of the Italian Line 1932–1977*. New York: Dover Publications Inc., 1999.

— *The QE2: A Picture History*. New York: Dover Publications Inc., 2008.

Robins, Nick. *The Decline and Revival of the British Passenger Fleet*. Newtownards, Northern Ireland: Colourpoint Books, 2001.

Shaum, Jack (editor). *Steamboat Bill*. East Providence, Rhode Island: Steamship Historical Society of America Inc., 1963–2010.

Wakefield, Iain (editor). *Ships Monthly*. Burton-on-Trent, Staffordshire, England, 1980–2010.